CAPITAL, DISTRIBUTION AND GROWTH:

A Look At Neo-Keynesian Economics

Stanley Bober
Professor of Economics
Duquesne University

To MARILYN

CONTENTS

At the time of writing this preface the American economy
does not present a very encouraging picture. It has entered
the 7th contraction of the post-world war II period, it remains
plagued by a high rate of inflation that is not expected to
be substantially moderated by the downturn, so that the
difficulty of stagflation will remain. And this is aggravated
by the inability of the nation to come to grips with the energy
problem; a problem that seems intractable as it becomes mired
in self-centered political outlook, and tragically as well, in a
lack of understanding of the workings of the market economy and
continuous utterings of demagoguery concerning profits and the
role of business generally.

The economy, in this summer of 1980, has not been the
inheritor of the results of a very happy business expansion.
This expansion (1975-1980) has not seen marked increases in
capacity and enhancement of productivity. There is evidence
that the economy has settled into a long-run productivity
outlook of less than 2% growth per annum. Productivity in the
nonfarm private sector fell from an average annual growth rate
of 2.7% during the period of 1948 to 1955, to an average rate
of 2.5% from 1955 to 1965, and to a rate of 2% from 1965 to 1973,
and dipping less than 1% from 1973 to 1977. This gloomy picture
becomes gloomier by seeing an output per hour growth of only .4%
in 1978, which is the smallest rise since the recession year of
1974. This "no growth" environment relates directly to the low
rates of business fixed investment. The real U.S. investment
growth rate in terms of an average of five years ending in 1968
was 8.0%, ending in 1973 it was 3.1% (with the corresponding real

G.N.P. growth rate being 3.3%), and ending in 1977 it was 1.7%
(with the real growth rate being 2.7%). Of course, this entire
problem has its basis in policies that stimulate demand and
retard savings. Consumer savings in the U.S. as a percentage
of disposable income (to look at one aspect of savings in the
economy) has fallen in the last decade, and fares quites badly
in a comparison with other industrialized countries, as the
following table shows:

	Rate of Saving	
	1977	1967
U.S.	5.1%	7.5%
Canada	9.8	6.2
Britain	13.9	8.5
West Germany	14.0	11.3
France	16.1	15.9
Japan	21.5	18.5

This is reflected in the figures for industrial production,
which over the decade from 1967 to 1977 shows a growth of about
40%; this is substantially below the gains for the other
industrialized countries (save for Britain which shows a smaller
gain).

Now on top of this relatively shrinking economic base we have
the constant increase in the government claim on resources, high
levels of transfer payments, a persistent high government deficit,
and a continuous increase in the money supply that exceeds the
real growth of the economy. With all of this, we still wonder why
our policy makers keep recocheting from one policy to another,
without making any progress towards the solution of the dual and
related problems of inflation and an erosion of economic growth.

Well, they are not really attacking the problem. They are
transfixed still by the post-war orthodoxy that the aim of policy
is to achieve "full-employment"; and to this end we have policies
that are greatly demand manipulating and income redistribution in effect.

The criterion for economic success seems not to be the growth
of economic resources, but some altered division of the given
"economic pie." Attention to the supply side of the equation
seems to have been submerged; with the ironic result that in
real terms a redistributive policy cannot in the long run be
effective, and full-employment will itself crumble.

But this orthodoxy based upon a simplistic view of Keynes'
work is still, in the main, at the core of macroeconomic
courses. The whole field of growth economics and that of the
neo-Keynesian paradigm remains outside the course offerings
at most institutions. Yet this work has beem percolating
in the profession for about 20 years. Must the lag be this
great between what is done at the research end and what is
taught in the classroom? It has got to be shortened if we are
to educate towards an understanding of our economic problems.
I hope that this book will play a role in altering the content
of the traditional macro course, and begin the necessary
wider exposure of the "new analytical framework" of post-
Keynesian thinking.

The design of the book runs as follows. In the first chapter
we present the neoclassical cost minimization-productivity approach
to production and distribution. In this we have a "rational"
explanation of matters but within a framework of a static economy.
In chapter 2 we show how this neoclassical approach is used to
forge a growth model that seems generally in line with the
characteristics of industrialized economies over the long-run. But
this explanation breaks down in vital areas, and in chapters 3-6
the book expounds on what is referred to as the Cambridge (England)
criticism of the neoclassical model. In these chapters there is an
examination of reswitching and related Wicksell effects. All this to
set the stage for the new macroeconomics - the neo-Keynesian model- in

chapters 7 and 8.

It is my belief that policies based on an understanding of
this new approach, and thereby having as its essential thrust that
of improving capital formulation and generating increased
productivity, would go far to alleviate some of the gloom mentioned
above. As an example, that investment is the key determinant of
economic growth, and that is is bound up with pricing and income
distribution; which brings us to what was said concerning redistribution
policies and the seemingly lack of attention paid to its effect on
production.

I wish to thank Margaret Barsh for typing the manuscript, and
for dealing smoothly with the many details that arise in seeing
the project to completion. To my wife Marilyn, to whom this book
is dedicated, a very special thanks for her continuous encouragement.
Her enthusiasm is that indispensible input.

July, 1980   Stanley Bober

1. PRODUCTION AND DISTRIBUTION
—THE TRADITIONAL STORY—

I

The firm seeks to adopt the least costly way of producing the amount of output it plans to sell. We identify two inputs that are capable of being varied in their application to produce output; that of labor services measured in man-hours, and that of capital measured in machine-hours. To avoid complications at the outset, let us accept that all of the labor and all of the capital are each of a uniform kind, capable of being related to each other in different quantities. Labor services are acquired by hiring workers and paying them a wage rate measured in dollars per man hour, and capital is acquired by, let us say, renting machines the cost of which can be thought of as a rental rate for a period of time.

There are two aspects of the decision concerning what combination of capital and labor will be employed. One of them is the purely physical side that deals with the degree of freedom available to the firm in being able to vary the proportion of capital to labor employed and still be capable of producing the desired level of output. We consider this first, and the look at the other financial side of the decision.

An isoquant is the name used by economists to describe the curve that traces out the alternative minimum combinations of capital and labor that yield the same level of output. Consider such a curve in fig. (1.1) where machine-hours (K) and labor hours (L) are measured on the vertical and horizontal axes respectively.

1

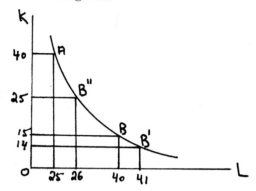

Fig. 1.1

Note the smooth contour of the curve, implying an infinite
number of different combinations of inputs to produce the
100 level of output; but to use the curve more realistically,
we can say that it implies the existence of a very "large"
number of productive techniques. The curve is negatively
sloped, telling us that as long as both inputs are used
efficiently, an additional unit of machine hours means
that less labor hours will be needed to produce the same
output. But the inward bending form of the isoquant (its
convexity) means that the amount of machine hours saved
due to the substitution of labor for capital becomes
increasingly less the greater the labor input (or conversely,
the less the capital input) when the substitution occurs.
Thus at point (A) with 25L and 40K, the productivity of
an additional unit of L is such that it is the equivalent of
15 units of K; but at point (B), given the employment of 40L
and 15K, the productivity of the 41st unit of L is such that it takes

2

the place of only one unit   of machine hours. The convexity
of the curve reflects the notion that the productivity of an
additional unit of labor (and by the term productivity we mean
here the amount of savings in machine hours that it gives
rise to) becomes less and less the greater the amount of labor
in use.

    This negative relation between the productivity of an
additional unit of the output (i.e. its marginal product) and
the amount of that input employed, is considered as the marginal
rate of technical substitution (MRTS). In more formal terms,
this MRTS measures the reduction in one input per unit change
(increase) in the other that is just sufficient to maintain a
constant level of output. It is, indeed, a measure of the rate
of substitution between the inputs at a point on the isoquant.
At point (A) the MRTS of labor for capital is 1 for 15 or the
equivalent of the reduction of 1 unit of (K) for every 1/15
unit of (L) additionally hired; but at point (B) the MRTS of
labor for capital is severely lessened to a rate of 1 labor
for 1 capital. Looking at this same matter from the opposite
side, we find that at point (B') an MRTS of capital for labor
of 1 for 1; but at point (B'') due to the greater productivity
of labor, the rate at which the two inputs may be substituted
for each other has greatly increased to 15 to 1.

    Should a point be reached where the capital employed is
at the necessary minimum with regard to the 100 level of output, the isoquant becomes parallel to the (L) axis; and for
the absolute minimum amount of (L) it becomes parallel to the
(K) axis with the (MRTS) being zero at these points.

    Fig. (1.2) illustrates a field of two isoquants with each,
as we now know, showing the alternative minimum mix of inputs
to produce the respective outputs. The firm may, in the

production of 100 units, decide on the (A) input combination;
or on a combination such as (A'). The point is, that while a
firm may err in employing excess factors (it is, in a physical
sense, wasting factors of production), it is prohibited from
employing an input combination that lies below the 100 level
isoquant by the technical relationship between input and output.

Fig. 1.2

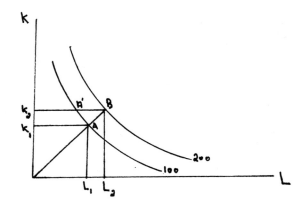

If the factor mix given by point (A) is chosen as representing
the least cost process, then the production of 200 output will
require that the level of employment of both capital and labor
rise, but that the ratio between them remain the same. We find
input ratios $\frac{OK_1}{OL_1} = \frac{OK_2}{OL_2}$. Thus a ray from the origin such as OAB

defines a constant capital/labor ratio, but where the magnitude
of the inputs along the ray increase. As contrasted with a
movement on the isoquant itself (along a ray one moves from
isoquant to isoquant) where it is the level of output that remains

4

constant, but the ratio of capital to labor producing this
output changes.

The extent of increase in factor magnitude as production
increases from point (A) to (B) in fig. (1.2) is a matter of
what is referred to as returns to scale. If all inputs where
to be increased in the same proportion, and this led to an
equal proportional increase in production, then the relationship between input and output is characterized by constant
returns to scale. This relationship will now be referred to
by the formal term of the production function; and with some
simple notation we write:

$$Y=F(K,L) \qquad 1.1$$

saying that the output level (Y) results from combining capital
and labor in some proportion. If (K) and (L) are doubled (Z=2)
and we can state:

$$ZY=F(ZK,ZL) \qquad 1.2$$

we have constant returns. Looking at this in term of the more
familiar output per unit of labor ratio, we note that changing
scale by increasing capital and labor proportionately has, in
this instance, no effect on the ratio $\frac{Y}{L}$. Should a doubling of
inputs lead to more than twice as much output we have increasing
returns to scale; and a situation of less than twice as much of
an output increase is referred to as decreasing returns to scale.

Before leaving these physical considerations, it will be
usefull for us to refocus our understanding of this MRTS, by
considering that the MRTS of capital for labor at a point on the
isoquant may also be expressed as the ratio of the marginal
product of labor to that of capital. It is simply another way
of using the concept of marginal product. Since an isoquant
represents a given level of production, then a move along the
curve, such as from (A) to (B'') on fig. (1.1) must tell us that

5

the loss in production caused by the reduction of 15K is entirely compensated by the increase in output due to the employment of an additional (L). One can write, as between any two points on the isoquant, that:

$$\Delta Y = MP_K \cdot \Delta K + MP_L \cdot \Delta L \quad 1.3$$

as $\Delta Y=0$, then:

$$0 = MP_k \cdot \Delta K + MP_L \cdot \Delta L$$

or

$$-\frac{\Delta K}{\Delta L} = \frac{MP_L}{MP_K} \quad 1.4$$

but $\frac{\Delta K}{\Delta L}$ is the slope of the curve, and the MRTS is the negative of this slope; thus:

$$MRTS = -\frac{\Delta K}{\Delta L} = \frac{MP_L}{MP_K} \quad 1.5$$

The goal of minimizing cost of production for a given output involves finding that physical input mix that is optimal, in the sense that it reflects the least expenditure. So that turning to the financial side of the discussion, let us suppose that the firm faces an existing wage rate (w) and rental rate (r). Its total cost for a mix of inputs is:

$$C = rK + wL \quad 1.6$$

Consider $r=\$10$ and $w=\$25$, then the possible combinations of inputs that can be purchased, say for an expenditure of $500, is:

$$500 = 10K+25L \quad 1.7$$

$$\text{and } K=50-2.5L \quad 1.8$$

Thus one can employ 50 machine hours and zero labor hours; and for every labor hour employed the firm would have to release 2.5 machine hours. The maximum amount of labor hours:

$$2.5L=50K$$

$$\text{with } K=0, \ L=20 \quad 1.9$$

6

Then for a cost of $500, the firm is able to employ 20L or 50K, or any combination of the two inputs within these limits. A curve that shows the combination of inputs that can be purchased for a given cost is labeled an isocost and depicted in fig. (1.3)

Fig. 1.3

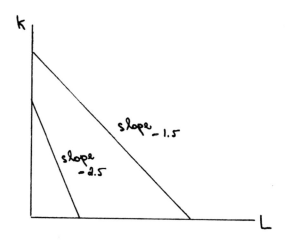

Note that the slope of the isocost reflects the relative prices of the inputs, and thus shows the extent to which the factor market permits the substitution of one factor for another. We can write an equation for the isocost curve as:

$$rK = C - wL \qquad 1.10$$
$$K = \frac{C}{r} - (\frac{w}{r})L$$

If L=O, the K=50, and for every unit increase in L, K declines by 2.5 (the slope of the curve is -2.5 or the negative of the ratio of input prices).

In fig. (1.4) we depict a field of two isocosts, one for each level of outlay; and while a higher outlay allows a greater total amount of factors to be employed, it does not alter the financial substitutability between them.

Fig. 1.4

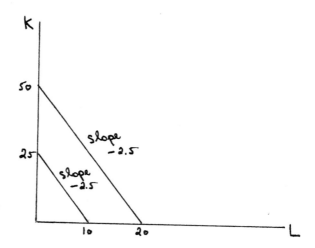

However, a change in relative factor prices for a given level of expenditure alters the slope of the same isocost line and affors the firm a new set of input possibilities. For example, assume the price of labor falls to 12 while that of capital falls to 8: then:

$$500=8K+12L$$
$$K=\frac{500}{8} - (\frac{12}{8})L \qquad 1.11$$

with K=62.5, L=0 and K=0, L=41.6. The slope of the isocost is

8

flatter being equal to -1.5. For every unit of labor that
the firm does not employ it can now hire 1.5 units of capital-
capital has become relatively more expensive. Previously the
value of a unit of capital was equivalent to less than 1/2 unit
value of labor, while now the value of a unit of capital is
equivalent to 2/3 that of labor. One would assume that the
firm would now try to seek a more labor using technique of
production. This condition is presented by the outer line in
fig. (1.3), where both lines depict the same isocost in
different price circumstances - not to be confused with fig.
(1.4), where we see different isocost lines for the same
factor price circumstance.

The firm is always operating under a combination of
financial and technical constraints with regard to its planned
level of production. It may enjoy little or no freedom in
varying its capital to labor input ratio, and from the cost
point of view it most likely faces mandated wage rates and rental
rates of capital. Within this framework, the firm seeks to
operate optimally, we can think of the firm as having to solve
an input choice for that combination of inputs that will
minimize production costs.

In fig. (1.5) we relate the constraints to each other.

Fig. 1.5

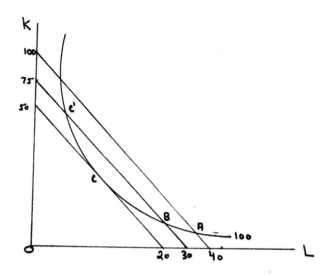

We have parallel isocost lines of the slope -2.5 and a production level of 100. Suppose we begin at point (A) where L_1 of labor and K_1 of capital are being utilized, summing to an expenditure of $1000. Can the firm, by taking advantage of its freedom to alter the combination of inputs reduce the cost of production? As we can see, if it switches the input mix from (A) to (B), the decline in the amount of labor is less than offset by the increase in machine hours; so that given the slope of the isocost, the firm ends up making a smaller total expenditure. We can say that the MRTS of capital for labor at point (A) is small

10

enough (reflecting the high marginal productivity of capital)
so as to reduce total costs.

As long as further substitutions of capital for labor
reduce costs, i.e. carries the firm to lower isocosts (such
as a further more from (B) to (C), these substitutions will
be made - assuming that the firm can do this and not cause a
loss in production. Note that at point (C) the firm realizes
the lowest cost possible for the 100 level of production;
further substitution will cause expenditures to rise. We are
saying that the MRTS of capital for labor at (C) is such that
in the move to (C') the increase in capital costs more than
offsets the decline in labor costs. It is at point (C) where
the slopes of the two constraint curves are equal, and it is
at this point that the firm can be said to be employing the
optimum combination of inputs. In other words, minimum cost
is realized when the MRTS of capital for labor is equal to
the ratio of the price of labor to the price of capital. Thus:

$$\frac{MP_L}{MP_K} = \frac{w}{r} \qquad 1.12$$

To reiterate: The left side of this equality tells the
producer the rate at which he can substitute capital for
labor in production, while the right side tells him the rate at
which he can substitute one for the other in the market place.

Consider the firm at point (C) reflecting the above
equality, and the suppose that due to some technical breakthrough, the productivity of a unit of capital rises, which
means that capital can now replace a greater number of units of
labor than previously - the left side of (1.12) is now lower
than the right side. It is as if we were back at point (B) in
fig. (1.5), where the slope of the isoquant is less than that
of the isocost. Lower costs can now be achieved by substituting

11

capital for labor. One would redraw fig. (1.5) showing an
optimum point (C) that reflects a greater proportion of
capital to labor, with the new isoquant being tangent to a
lower isocost line. The MRTS between inputs is then defined
for the technology at a point in time; and the firm seeks
that input mix which, for the given technology and prices, is
least cost.

Let us supply some numbers to this. Suppose point (C)
reflects an equality of:

$$\frac{50}{20} = \frac{25}{10} \quad (\frac{MP_L}{MP_K} = \frac{w}{r}) \qquad\qquad 1.13$$

which can be put as:

$$\frac{50}{25} = \frac{20}{10} \quad (\frac{MP_L}{w} = \frac{MP_K}{r}) \qquad\qquad 1.14$$

telling us that the ratio of labor's contribution to
production to its price is identical to that of capital;
in simpler terms, the return for each dollar spent on
capital and labor is the same. One cannot improve one's
optimum position (considered here as attaining a greater
production level for the same cost) by altering the proportion
of capital to labor in production.

However, should a change occur in the productivity of
capital as to alter the left side of (1.13) to read $\frac{50}{25}$, then
we have:

$$\frac{50}{25} < \frac{25}{10} \quad (\frac{MP_L}{w} < \frac{MP_K}{r}) \qquad\qquad 1.15$$

The addition to production per dollar spent on capital exceeds
that spent on labor, so that by employing one less labor unit
and this switching to 2 1/2 additional units of capital, total
production goes up by 12.5. In other words for the same
expenditure, the firm realizes greater output by substituting
capital for labor.

But the need to alter the input mix may flow as well
from a change in the price of the inputs. Using the outer
isocost line in fig. (1.3) with a slope of -1.5, we see
that the prices of both inputs have fallen, but that of labor
more so than capital. Our ratio statement now reads:

$$\frac{50}{20} > \frac{12}{8} \qquad\qquad 1.16$$

or

$$\frac{50}{12} > \frac{20}{8} \; (\frac{MP_L}{w} > \frac{MP_K}{r})$$

The ratio of production of labor to its cost is now greater than
that of capital; so that moving to an optimum (considered here
as attaining the lowest cost for a given output level) involves
the substitution of labor for capital. The firm ends up
spending less to produce the same level of output if it uses
more labor.

II

There is no dount that input price changes occur frequently,
and we must continue to be sensitive to the influence of such
changes (as well as changes in factor productivity) on the
selection of the production technology, and ultimately on the
shares of the rewards of production going to capital and labor.
We now want to clarify the connection between this rational and
cost-minimizing behavior of the producing (employing) unit of
the economy and the distribution of income among inputs.

As necessary background, we look at the marginal productivity
theory of input pricing which sets forth a fundamental tenet of
a market economy, to the effect that inputs receive compensation
in an amount determined by their contribution to output. There
is indeed, a natural basis for determining a "just" income.

We utilize a single variable production function which

13

depicts output as a function of labor input, with the level
of capital held constant ($\bar{K}$). Thus:

$$Y=F(L,\bar{K}) \qquad 1.17$$

The shape of this function in fig. 1.16 shows that, initially,
output increases at an increasing rate with the injection of
labor to the fixed capital stock; at the beginning, capital
per man is high. But after some level of employment (L_1) output
begins to increase at a decreasing rate as the capital stock is
spread over more and more men. Here we find decreasing
marginal returns to output; and at some future level of employment a point may be reached where no additions to output would
result from added employment.

Fig. 1.6

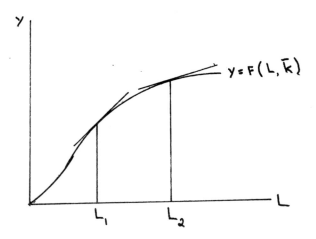

From this configuration of the output function, we can derive
the movement in the average product of labor (AP_L) - the ratio of

14

output produced to labor employed $(\frac{Y}{L})$; and also of the marginal
product of labor $(\frac{\Delta Y}{\Delta L}$ or $^{MP}L)$. As employment increases, the
average product rises as output increases by more than the
increase in employment; this is due to the circumstance that
additions to employment will cause production to rise by more
than the average product of the previous level of employment.
At the maximum average product of labor, we see that $MP_L = AP_L$;
additions to employment beyond this point causes AP_L to fall
as a result of $MP_L < AP_L$. Fig. (1.7) shows the movements in
the MP_L and the AP_L.

Fig. 1.7

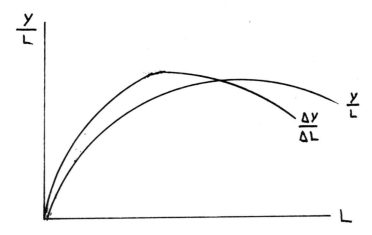

Such then is the blueprint for production when the firm is able
to vary a single input, and though we talk in terms of labor, the
same result emerges from varying the capital input while holding
labor constant.

15

Let us now look at a tabular expression.

Table 1.1

Labor Input	Total Output	Marginal Product	Price per unit Output	Value of Marginal Product	Price per unit of labor
0	–	–	–	–	–
1	15	15	20	300	50
2	31	16	20	320	50
3	43	12	20	240	50
4	51	8	20	160	50
5	55	4	20	80	50
6	57	2	20	40	50
7	58	1	20	20	50

We assume that the firm can sell its output at a given price
of $20 per unit, and also faces a given price per unit of
labor of $50, which is unaffected by the number of units
it wishes to employ. The task of the firm is to find
that level of employment (and correspondingly that level
of production) which maximizes its profit. The entry in
column (5) is the contribution to total production of
that added labor input multipled by the selling price per
unit of that added production. In other words, it is the
revenue from employing an additional unit of labor.

While the addition to the firm's income reaches a
maximum with the employment of the second unit of labor,
this does not imply that profits are simultaneously at a
maximum. Since the value of the marginal product of the
third unit of labor is 240 and its cost is 50, an
additional profit of 190 is realized from its employ.

16

The firm will continue to add to employment and production as long, as in doing so, it also adds to profits - in our example, through the fifth unit of labor. One would normally state this as follows: that the firm will continue to hire labor up to the point where the net revenue of the labor hired equals its cost. So that if labor could be applied in a continuous fashion (using the derivative notion) rather than in discrete units, we can splice in as much labor as we need between the fifth and sixth unit, and hence cause the marginal product to fall continuously to the point where net revenue is zero. Given the particular product and resource prices, the increase in profits at each level of employment depends on the resulting increase in output; which in turn depends upon the technology embodied in the capital stock with which labor interacts, as well as the skill brought by the labor units themselves.

Table (1.2) illustrates the same principle, but with higher levels of labor productivity, and we note that employment is now extended to 7 units.

Table 1.2

Labor Input	Total Output	Marginal Product	Price per Unit Output	Value of Marginal Product	Price per Unit of labor
0	-	-	-	-	-
1	25	25	20	500	50
2	45	20	20	400	50
3	61	16	20	320	50
4	73	12	20	240	50
5	81	8	20	160	50
6	85	4	20	80	50
7	88	3	20	60	50
8	90	2	20	40	50

The point to be made is that an increase in the productivity of labor (at the given price of labor) will make it worthwhile for the firm to increase employment.

The principle gleaned from our variable factor case, is that the optimum employment of the factor is at the level where the additional revenue obtained is equal to its cost of employment. That is:[1]

$$p \cdot \frac{dY}{dL} = w \qquad 1.18$$

p = Price per unit of output

We have rational behavior on the part of the firm which, at the same time as it maximizes profits, determines employment levels and the share of output going to labor. Note that equation (1.18) is simply the expression for the numerator of both sides of equation (1.12), with the assumption p=1; the flow is from the behavior of the firm to income distribution. In table 1.1 the firm produces $1100 worth of output with $250 going to labor; in table 1.2 we find a profit maximizing value of output of $1850 with total wages equalling $400. While total wages are higher due to the higher level of employment, we find that wages as a proportion of the value of production falls from 23% to 22%; but note that table 1.2 carries the not too likely supposition that the wage rate of labor does not change, as the demand for labor increases due to the increase in its productivity.

Now let us move a further step and say that the firm can vary the quantity of capital as well as that of labor. If we are going to vary the capital input, we than also have to reckon with changes in its marginal productivity as it interacts with more or less labor.

To start matters, assume that the firm is expanding production and realizing increasing profits by increasing

18

the labor input rather than by adding to the capital stock.
Such an action carries with it the inevitable result of
lessening the very increase in profits that motivated it.
There will emerge the combined outcomes of an increase in
the price of labor resulting from its higher demand, and the
technical effect of a lessening in the productivity of additional
inputs of labor, as labor finds itself insufficiently complemented
by units of capital. Assuming a given selling price of
output, the excess of the value of the marginal product of
labor over its cost will narrow, paving the way for a more
profitable mode of production - one that entails the use of
a greater number of units of capital.

An increase in the value of the marginal product of
capital and hence in the profitability of its employment will,
at some point in the input mix decision, cause the firm to
increase the capital input. It is realistic to presume that
the firm is always seeking the best level of capital to
complement its labor force, as well as the reverse. But the
same inevitability of result will also affect the increase
in profits from the heightened use of the capital factor.
What we are getting at, is that as long as it is more
profitable to switch from one input ration to another, the
move will be made. When both factors are equally profitable
to employ the firm finds its least cost ratio, we are at ratio
(1.14). And unless further changes occur in prices or
productivity, the firm can be expected to expand production with
that particular ratio. It is via this decision in seeking the
least cost point - and we can aggregate our thinking and say on
the part of all firms - that one can make a statement about the
distribution of income among factor inputs.

19

Maximization of profits entails:

$$r = p \cdot \frac{dY}{dK} \quad \text{and} \quad rK = p \cdot \frac{dY}{dK} \cdot K \qquad 1.19$$

$$w = p \cdot \frac{dY}{dL} \quad \text{and} \quad wL = p \cdot \frac{dY}{dL} \cdot L$$

We can then express factor shares as:

$$\frac{rK}{Y} = \frac{\frac{dY}{dK} \cdot K}{Y} \qquad 1.20$$

$$\frac{wL}{Y} = \frac{\frac{dY}{dL} \cdot L}{Y}$$

For a given level of output, the proportion of the value of that output going to labor and capital depends on the number of the factor employed and its marginal productivity.

The lower the price of a factor relative to its productivity, the greater the number of units employed; and, to the extent that technical considerations allow, this will also affect the employment of the other factor input. It then follows that we should be able to set down a guide to changes in the distribution of income when there are changes in the input price ratio. Such a guide is the elasticity of substitution, which is a measure of the percentage change in the actual proportion of use of the inputs in response to a given percentage change in the MRTS. We recall that the MRTS is a measure of the rate of change in the proportion between inputs; hence:

$$MRTS = \frac{MP_L}{MP_K} \qquad 1.21$$

and in the least cost position:

$$MP_L = \frac{w}{p} \qquad 1.22$$

$$MP_K = \frac{r}{p}$$

20

Therefore, we can write the elasticity of substitution (σ) as:

$$\sigma = \frac{\%\Delta(\frac{K}{L})}{\%\Delta(\frac{W}{r})} \qquad 1.23$$

The relation between the elasticity of substitution and input shares is summarized in table 1.3.

Table 1.3

$\Delta(\frac{W}{r})$	Change in Factor Shares ↑ increase ↓ decrease → no change		
	$\sigma > 1$	$\sigma = 1$	$\sigma < 1$
$(\frac{W}{r})$ Increases	Labor ↓	Labor →	Labor ↑
	Capital ↑	Capital →	Capital ↓
$(\frac{W}{r})$ Decreases	Labor ↑	Labor →	Labor ↓
	Capital ↓	Capital →	Capital ↑

III

The particular form of the production function that can be used to underpin our discussion of the distribution of income is that of the Cobb-Douglas. While we have touched upon the relationship between inputs and outputs before, it now seems appropriate to set down the entire matter of the production function in some detail, since it is a necessary vehicle to explore many points.

We repeat equation (1.1):

$$Y = F(K,L) \qquad 1.24$$

and can say that the effect on total production of an addition to capital and labor is positive; and as a consequence of diminishing returns we will see decreasing

21

increments to the output flow resulting from the application
of either input. All this, though familiar to us at this
point, can be put in a more exact form as:

$$\frac{dY}{dK} > 0, \ \frac{dY}{dL} > 0 \qquad\qquad 1.25$$

and

$$\frac{d^2Y}{dK^2} < 0, \ \frac{d^2Y}{dL^2} < 0$$

The function is defined as linear homogeneous if F(ZK,ZL) =
ZF(K,L) for any combination of K and L, and for any value of
(Z). Should the inputs be increased in the proportion (Z)
and output alos increased in the proportion (Z), then the
function is homogeneous of the degree unity. Should output
increase in a proportion greater than (Z), then the function
shows increasing returns to scale, or, is said to be homogeneous of degree greater than unity.

Translating the function into the Cobb-Douglas form, we
write:

$$Y = K^{\alpha} L^{1-\alpha} \qquad\qquad 1.26$$

where the exponents (α) and ($1-\alpha$) are positive functions that
add to one. We need to show that the constants (α) and ($1-\alpha$)
are the output elasticities of capital and labor. The output
elasticity with regard to capital is:

$$\frac{\frac{dY}{Y}}{\frac{dk}{K}} = \frac{dY}{Y} \cdot \frac{K}{dK} \qquad\qquad 1.27$$

and from (1.26):

$$\frac{dY}{dK} = \alpha K^{\alpha-1} L^{1-\alpha} \qquad\qquad 1.28$$

22

then substituting into (1.27):

$$\frac{K\alpha K^{\alpha-1} L^{1-\alpha}}{K^\alpha L^{1-\alpha}} = \frac{\alpha K^{\alpha-1} K}{K^\alpha} = \alpha \qquad 1.29$$

And by the same method it may be seen that:

$$\frac{dY}{Y} \cdot \frac{L}{dL} = 1-\alpha \qquad 1.30$$

Also (α) and $(1-\alpha)$ represent the relative shares of capital
and labor in output. From (1.20) we have:

$$\frac{rK}{Y} = \frac{dY}{\frac{dK}{Y}} \cdot K \qquad 1.31$$

then: $\quad \dfrac{rK}{Y} = \dfrac{\alpha K^{\alpha-1} L^{1-\alpha} K}{K^\alpha L^{1-\alpha}} = \dfrac{\alpha K^\alpha L^{1-\alpha}}{K^\alpha L^{1-\alpha}} = \alpha$

And similarly, labor's share is $(1-\alpha)$.

An additional feature of the Cobb-Douglas is that it is
characterized by an elasticity of substitution equal to unity.
We can express equation (1.23) as:

$$\frac{d(\frac{K}{L})}{d(\frac{w}{r})} \cdot \frac{\frac{w}{r}}{\frac{K}{L}} \qquad 1.32$$

and we know that:

$$\frac{w}{r} = \frac{MP_L}{MP_K} = \frac{(1-\alpha)K^\alpha L^{-\alpha}}{\alpha K^{\alpha-1} L^{1-\alpha}} \qquad 1.33$$

setting in terms of $k=\dfrac{K}{L}$:

$$\frac{w}{r} = \frac{(1-\alpha) k^\alpha}{\alpha(k)^{\alpha-1}} = \frac{1-\alpha}{\alpha} (k) \qquad 1.34$$

then:

$$\frac{d(k)}{d(\frac{1-\alpha}{\alpha}k)} \cdot \frac{\frac{1-\alpha}{\alpha} k}{k} = 1 \qquad 1.35$$

Should the Cobb-Douglas be a fair representation of the productive
relationships of the economy, then a rise in the capital to labor

ratio will be associated with a constancy in capital's
relative income share. What we have in this σ measure is a
statement about the ease of substitution of capital for labor.
If it is zero, inputs cannot be substituted for each other;
we have fixed input proportions. If it is infinity, the factors
are perfect substitutes for each other. A measure of unity
means they are sufficiently substitutible, so that a change in
the input price ratio has no effect on the distribution of
income.

IV

We cannot presume that the injection of factors to the
productive process occurs within a given technological framework. Certainly the productivity of an input is constantly
being acted upon by improvements in technology which, for
example, may allow a greater amount of output for the same
batch of inputs. One can conceive of this happening due to
organizational changes within the firm; or that the given
input ratio becomes more productive due to the experience
acquired because of prolonged doing. Of course, the act of
increasing the capital stock cannot be presumed to mean that
of the same type of capital. As we will come to see when we
get into this matter, technological change becomes infused into
the productive process via the act of accumulation of capital.
For now, we want to see, somewhat more precisely, how we can
reckon with the effect of technological change on the distribution of income.

Neutral technical progress describes a situation where the
firm can produce the same level of output with fewer inputs
(or a greater output with the same inputs); but where such an
increased capability results from the fact that the productivity

of labor and capital have increased to the same degree. At the
given capital to labor ratio, an invention is incorporated into
the productive process that leaves unchanged the ratio of the
marginal product of labor to that of capital. And, as the
economically efficient operation implies that inputs are paid
their productivity, then the ratio of input payments, and hence
the share of capital and labor in output remains unchanged.
Neutral progress leaves unchanged the MRTS between capital and
labor. We see this in figure (1.8) where this technological
change is represented by a shift of the isoquant towards the
origin.

Fig. 1.8

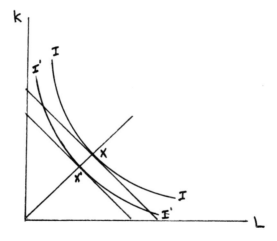

Isoquants II and I'I' represent the same level of output, and
the slopes of both curves are the same at the existing capital to
labor ratio.

25

But this can be handled with greater flexibility by writing:
$$Y = A(t)F(K,L) \qquad 1.36$$
or, in its Cobb-Douglas form:
$$Y = Ae^{nt} K^{\alpha} L^{1-\alpha} \qquad 1.37$$

The (A) term is an index of technical change, where A=1 at t=0 and $\frac{dA}{dt} > 0$ at some rate (n) for all t>0. There is an upward drift of output at a rate per unit of time for a given input ratio.

We can restate the production function on a per capita basis by letting Z=1/L which implies that the function works with one unit of labor. Then:
$$\frac{Y}{L} = F(\frac{1}{L} \cdot K, \frac{1}{L} \cdot L) \qquad 1.38$$

$$\frac{Y}{L} = f\ (\frac{K}{L},1)$$

or   y=f(k)

saying that output per unit of labor is a function of capital per unit of labor. And, in the absence of technological change, increasing the degree of capital intensity would have output per unit of labor behave in accordance with the configuration of figure (1.6). Neutral progress in this context can be written as:
$$y = Ae^{nt}\ f(k) \qquad 1.39$$
and diagrammatically:

Fig. 1.9

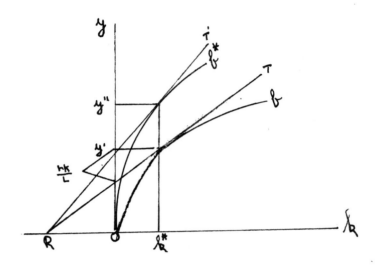

There is the production function (f); and (f*) is derived from
(f) by measuring output per head for a given capital per head.
Relative shares can be read from figure (1.9). We have:

$$y = f(k)$$
$$\text{then: } L \cdot \frac{Y}{L} = Lf(\frac{K}{L}) = Lf(k) \qquad 1.40$$
$$\text{so: } Y = Lf(k)$$

As the rate of profit is taken equal to the marginal
product of capital, we can write:

$$r = \frac{dY}{dK} = Lf'(\frac{K}{L}) \cdot \frac{1}{L} \qquad 1.41$$
$$= f'(k)$$

The rate of profit is the slope of the per unit labor production
function. The wage rate being equal to the marginal product of
labor is:

27

$$w = \frac{dY}{dL} = -kf'(k) + f(k) \qquad 1.42$$

Given the particular k=k*, output per man on function (f) is
y', with profits per man being:

$$(\frac{K^*}{L}) \cdot r \ [\equiv f'(k)] \qquad 1.43$$

At point (k*) the rate of profit will be given by the slope
of the function represented by the tangent (RT) drawn to the
function at that point. Thus profits per unit of labor are given
by the difference between (y') and the intercept of the tangent
to the function. For a given (k*) we have a particular distribution of income; wages per capita being the difference between
(y') and profits per capita.

The function (f*) demonstrates the rise in output per unit
of labor to (y"); with the tangent (RT') showing the equi-
proportionate rise in the productivity of capital and labor. The
rise in profits per unit of labor and wages per unit of labor
are in proportion to the rise in (y) maintaining the given
distribution of income (as shown by the distance (OR).

We turn to another type of technical change classified as
capital using (labor saving). At the existing capital to labor
ratio ther is a development which raises the ratio of the
marginal product of capital to that of labor. Figure 1.10
illustrates this change in the same manner as before by a shift
of the isoquant towards the origin.

Fig. 1.10

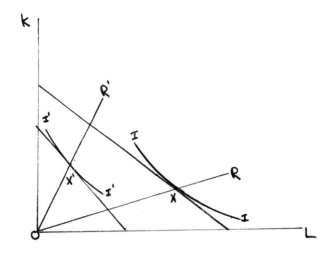

The original input mix is given by the ray OR reflecting
the particular equality of the MRTS and the input price ratio
at point X. But this type of change will cause the firm to
substitute the more productive capital for labor in producing
the same output level. Note that the slope of the isoquant
is flatter at X' than at X; a smaller increase in the units of
capital employed now compensates for a unit reduction in labor
employed. This technical progress results in a fall in the
ratio (w/r) reflecting the increase in capital's share in
output. And this prompts the move to utilize more of the
factors whose share has risen due to its improved productivity;
the firm swings over to a ray depicting this changed input mix.

By similar reasoning we identify a labor using (capital

saving) technical change as one where at the given capital to labor ratio, the marginal product of labor rises relative to capital, with an increase in the ratio of (w/r). This change is seen in figure 1.11. Note that the I'I' isoquant is steeper, showing that fewer units of labor need now compensate for a given reduction in capital.

Fig. 1.11

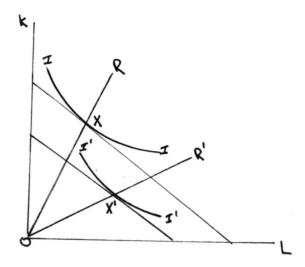

Technological change can be assessed in terms of elasticity of output. The output elasticity of labor can be expressed as the ratio of the value of the marginal product of labor to the average value of the amount of labor employed. Thus:

$$\frac{\frac{dY}{dL}}{\frac{Y}{L}} = 1-\alpha \qquad 1.44$$

30

Inverting the left side of statement (1.44) gives the familiar elasticity measure:

$$\frac{L}{Y} \cdot \frac{dY}{dL} \qquad\qquad 1.45$$

Technological progress is neutral if the output elasticity of labor (and also that of capital) remains constant — that is, output elasticity of a factor and its relative share are identical. For the case of labor we have:

$$\frac{dY}{dL} = 1-\alpha \; K^{\alpha}L^{\,1-\alpha-1} \qquad\qquad 1.46$$

and

$$\frac{dY}{dL} \cdot \frac{L}{Y} = \frac{1-\alpha K^{\alpha}L^{1-\alpha-1}L}{K^{\alpha}L^{1-\alpha}} = 1-\alpha$$

total labor income (W) = L $\cdot$ w or L $\cdot \dfrac{dY}{dL}$

then W = L $\cdot$ 1$-\alpha K^{\alpha}L^{1-\alpha-1}$ = 1$-\alpha K^{a}L^{1-\alpha}$ = $(1-\alpha)Y$

and $1-\alpha \cong \dfrac{W}{Y}$ \qquad\qquad 1.47

Repeating the case of capital:

Profits (K$\cdot$r) = K $\cdot \dfrac{dY}{dK}$

$= K\alpha K^{\alpha-1} \, L^{1-\alpha} = \alpha K^{\alpha}L^{1-\alpha} = \alpha Y$ \qquad\qquad 1.48

and $\alpha = \dfrac{Kr}{Y}$

Now that we have set out the basic form of neo-classical theory, we will in the following chapters subject it to some critical inquiry. But first, we move to place this form within the framework of a growing economy.

1. The incentive to increase employment is present when
    dR>0 (R=net revenue) which means that $p \cdot \frac{dY}{dL} - w>0$. The
    firm hires to the point where dR=0 or $p \cdot \frac{dY}{dL} = W$. Another
    way to look at this is to understand that the production
    function now reads Y=F(L) with R=pY - wL. Differentiating
    with respect to L and equating to zero gives:

$$\frac{dR}{dL} = p \frac{dY}{dL} - w = 0$$

and $\quad p \frac{dY}{dL} = w$

2. A NEOCLASSICAL GROWTH MODEL

I

In this chapter we construct a growth model using the neoclassical ingredients.[1] We deal with a growing economy that predictably sets aside a certain proportion of its output for capital accumulation. When this economy settles into its steady-state condition (when it exhbits a constant proportional rate of growth) it will be able, from the proportion of its output that is invested, to equip the new entrance to the labor force with the same level of capital per worker as that of the existing work force. That is, in a steady-state condition, the economy exhbits a constant capital to labor ratio.

Furthermore, our approach is at the highest level of aggregation, in that the economy is composed of a single sector producing a single output that is an all purpose good. This good is consumed, and that portion of it that is not so used (i.e. saved) is accumulated and increases the capital stock. There is no need in this setup to work up behavioral functions for investment demand and savings; the act of savings is the equivalent act of investment. Putting this another way, we can say that investment intentions are always brought into harmony with desired savings, and desired savings are always realized. There is also no concern with relative prices of output, nor with any notion of different kinds of capital that may be appropriate to different capital/output ratios (different techniques of production).

Our single kind of capital is perfectly malleable; it can be squeezed up or down to work with greater or lesser

33

amounts of labor, it is the same capital regardless of
factor proportions in its use. This capital instantaneously
alters its shape for all of its self to the kind of capital
that is required to operate most profitably at a particular
capital/labor ratio. Various metaphorical devices have been
employed to convey the appropriate flavor of fantasy to this
notion. We may find references in the literature to putty,
leets, meccano sets, corn and cows (which may be eaten or used
to produce more cows).

Can this approach characterized by a single homogeneous
capital good and a production function that allows continuous
factor substitution serve as a parable? Can the operation
of such a model serve to illuminate what is happening in the
real world?

The model is constructed upon:

i. An assumption that the labor force is
growing exogenously at a rate (λ). Thus:

$$L_T = L_0 e^{\lambda t} \qquad 2.1$$

ii. The continuous form production function
translated into the Cobb-Douglas:

$$Y = K^\alpha L^{1-\alpha} \qquad 2.2$$

and put into per capita form:

$$y = k^\alpha \qquad 2.3$$

iii. The change in the capital stock is a
function in the level of output:

$$\frac{dK}{dt} \equiv I_t = S_t = sY_t \qquad 2.4$$

assuming here that capital does not
depreciate so that all investment is simply
the rate of increase to the capital stock.

The relation between output per capita and capital per
capita is depicted in figure (2.1) showing diminishing

returns to increases in (k) - as we expect from the characteristics of this production function. Thus the marginal
product of increases in (k) is:

$$MP_k = \frac{dy}{dk} = \alpha k^{\alpha-1} \qquad 2.5$$

with the increase to the rate of increase being negative:

$$\frac{d^2y}{dk^2} = \alpha(\alpha-1)k^{\alpha-2} \qquad 2.6$$

$$(\alpha<1)$$

Fig. 2.1

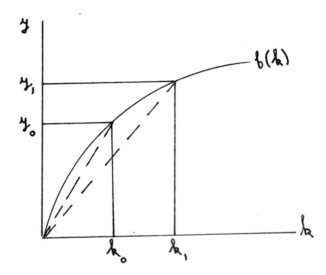

It is interesting to note that the slope of a line drawn from the
origin to a point on the function is a measure of the inverse of
the capital to output ratio (k/y = V) at that point. At point

35

(k_o) we have a ratio y_o/k_o or $1/V_o$; an increase to (k_1) causes a smaller proportionate increase to (y_1), thus y_1/k_1 or $1/V_1$, and the slope showing $\frac{1}{V_1} < \frac{1}{V_o}$. We have a function that shows increases in the ratio of capital to output as the economy accumulates capital and increases the ratio of capital to labor.

II

Given these operational tools and assumptions, we can go ahead and demonstrate the fundamental outcome of the model; that for a given growth of the labor force the economy will always generate a rate of growth of the capital stock equal to that of the labor force, and hence maintain full-employment of the growing labor supply. From whatever the initial rate of accumulation, there is an internal mechanism tending towards that rate of capital growth which keeps constant the capital/labor ratio, and thereby keeps constant the ratios of output per unit of labor and that of capital to output. There is an inherent tendency towards a steady-state solution where all variables exhibit a constant rate of increase equal to the exogenous rate of growth of the labor force.

A view of this outcome is:

i. $\quad \dfrac{dK}{dt} \equiv \dot{K} = s(Y)$ $\qquad\qquad$ 2.7

ii. $\quad Y = K^{\alpha}L^{1-\alpha}$

iii. $\quad \dot{K} = s(K^{\alpha}L^{1-\alpha})$

iv. $\quad L = L_0 e^{\lambda t}$

v. $\quad \dot{K} = s\,[K^{\alpha}\,(L_0 e^{\lambda t})^{1-\alpha}]$

Knowing the savings rate and thus the level of investment, and also the labor supply, we "compute" from the production function the full employment level of output. And for that given (s) and

(λ) all future output is so computed, as equations (2.7ii) and (2.7iv) are identified in (2.7v). Equation (2.7v) tells us the level of investment out of a full-employment level of output which, with the given labor supply, will maintain such levels into the future. Having set the system on the full employment output track, given the appropriate savings propensity, it will stay there – exhibiting a constant (y) as a function of a constant (k).

Another view on a per unit of labor basis can be seen as:

i. $k = \dfrac{K}{L}$ 2.8

ii. $\dfrac{\dot{k}}{k} = \dfrac{\dot{K}}{K} - \dfrac{\dot{L}}{L}$

iii. $\dfrac{\dot{k}}{k} = \dfrac{\dot{K}}{K} - \lambda$

iv. $\dot{k} = k\dfrac{\dot{K}}{K} - k\lambda$

v. $\dot{K} = sF(K,L)$

vi. $\dot{k} = \dfrac{ksF(K,L)}{K} - k\lambda$

vii. $\dot{k} = ksf(1,\tfrac{1}{k}) - k\lambda$

viii. and $\dot{k} = sf(k) - k\lambda$

or

ix. $\dfrac{\dot{k}}{k} \equiv \hat{k} = \dfrac{sf(k)}{k} - \lambda$

Given (s), there is a particular (k) and hence a particular (y) that results in a rate of accumulation such that $\dot{k} = 0$. Or, using (2.8ix) it is better to talk in terms of a zero rate of change in the capital/labor ratio which is given for a particular capital/output ratio, as the first term on the right side of (2.8ix) is $s(\tfrac{1}{K/y})$.

Operationally, we can view the adjustment of the economy to its equilibrium (steady-state) condition in figure (2.2).

Fig. 2.2

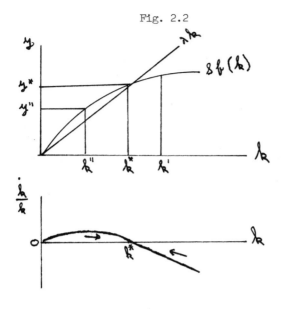

As we indicated, the equilibrium capital to labor ratio is that value of the ratio which makes the rate of change in the ratio equal to zero. By setting (2.8ix) equal to zero, we have:

$$\frac{sf(k)}{k} = \lambda \qquad\qquad 2.9$$

or

$$sf(k) = \lambda k$$

which is saying that output per capita is such as to yield a rate of investment [s(y)] equal to that which keeps constant the capital/labor ratio; equal to (λk) which defines the steady-state (k), i.e. k*.

Starting at k = k" and y = y" then, given (s), we have a

38

rate of accumulation exceeding that of the labor force, resulting in $\hat{k} > 0$ (a state of capital deepening) and thereby causing output per capita to increase. But this rate of capital deepening will bring into being conditions that will, over time, cause this deepening rate itself to diminish; for past some point it will lead to an increase in output per capita that is proportionately smaller than the growth in per capita capital. When that happens, for the given savings ratio, the rate of growth in capital per head will decline. Starting from a point to the left of k^*, the economy moves towards k^*; a too rapid rate of capital accumulation is self-correcting via diminishing returns to output.

We should also bear in mind that as the system adjusts from k'', it is characterized by an increasing ratio of capital to output. The steady-state condition is given for a particular capital/output ratio (V^*) corresponding to (k^*). We can write expression (2.9) as:

$$\frac{\lambda}{s} = \frac{f(k^*)}{k^*} = \frac{1}{V^*} \qquad 2.10$$

and

$$V^* = \frac{s}{\lambda}$$

The particular V^* is not a technological given assumption of the model; it is the outcome of an adjusting process of the economy that has a given (s) and (λ).

At $k = k'$ the generated investment is not sufficient to keep the capital stock growing at the same rate as the labor force. We have:

$$\frac{sf(k)}{k} < \lambda \qquad 2.11$$

But this condition of a too small a rate of accumulation will cause, at some point, an increasing ratio of output to capital. This will subsequently turn conditions around

by increasing the level of capital and that of output per
capita more than proportionately and thus the negative growth
to the capital/labor ratio. Thus the economy returns to
k^*, y^*; and the trip back is characterized by a falling
capital/output ratio. In this sequence output and capital
grow at faster and faster rates, enabling them to equal
that of (λ); whereas, starting from k'', output and capital
grow at smaller rates as they fall to the (λ) rate.

We can express these movements, perhaps more vividly,
in terms of the productivities of the inputs. At k',
for example, the presence of a "high" capital/labor ratio
indicates that the marginal product of labor will be rising
relative to that of capital; and, in line with our
discussion in chapter 1 will cause a switch-over to less
capital using techniques. But this action reduces the
rate of growth of capital. The use of those techniques
which causes the rate of growth of output to decline, also
reduces the savings (surplus) per worker available for
capital deepening. But this is self-correcting; for when
the rate of accumulation falls below that of the labor
force, it begins to generate increasing returns.

Another way to depict the equilibrium growth
condition is to write:
$$\hat{Y} = \alpha\hat{K} + (1-\alpha) \lambda \qquad\qquad 2.12$$
where, as we showed in Chapter 1, the (α) and ($1-\alpha$) are the
output elasticities of capital and labor. Then:
$$\hat{Y} - \lambda = \alpha(\hat{K}-\lambda) \qquad\qquad 2.13$$
telling us that the growth in output per unit of labor is
equal to the growth in capital per unit of labor multiplied
by its "marginal product". In equilibrium, $\hat{Y} = \lambda$ as
$\hat{K} = \lambda$ ($\equiv k^*$).

III

Let us now restate the equilibrium condition, so that we can focus on another point. Thus:

$$\frac{sf(k^*)}{k^*} = \lambda \qquad\qquad 2.14$$

or

$$s(y^*) = \lambda k^*$$

and

$$y^* = \frac{\lambda}{s} \ (k^*)$$

The question is, what is the effect on the equilibrium growth rate of an increase in the savings ratio? The immediate effect is to go to a condition where:

$$y > \frac{\lambda}{s} \ (k^*) \qquad\qquad 2.15$$

Investment will now be growing at a faster rate than the labor force which initially produces a rate of growth in (y) that exceeds the growth rate in (k). But this higher rate of accumulation must eventually result in diminishing returns to output per capita which reduces the very rate of increase in capital itself. When the ratio (y) is drawn down sufficiently to compensate for the increase in the savings rate, the output to capital ratio will be such as to result — for this higher savings rate — in a rate of capital growth that is once again equal to that of the labor force. When (k) stops rising, it is an indication that the economy has accommodated to the higher savings rate; and this accumulation is, so to speak, reflected in the existence of a now higher capital to output ratio.

An increase in the savings rate will, for a time, cause output and capital to grow at a greater rate than the labor force; but this is a transitory period as the economy adjusts from one steady-state growth condition to another. Thus despite an increase in the propensity to save, the long-run

41

(when the economy settles into the steady-state) growth of output and capital is still what is was prior to the increase - that of the exogenously given (λ) rate. We see this in figure (2.3)

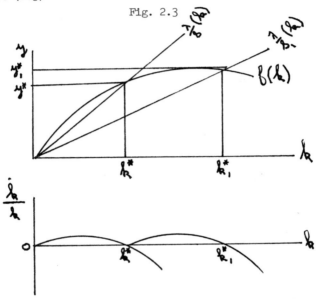

Fig. 2.3

The increase in the savings rate from s to s_1 flattens the slope of the λ/s line and rotates it to the right. This shows the initial increase in (k) that results in a more than proportionate increase in (y) that in turn kicks the (k) up further. But the rise in the growth rate of output lessens over time, thereby reducing the growth in capital as the economy settles to the k^*_1, y^*_1 position.

42

As a k* position can be given in terms of a particular capital/output ratio (V), we can show the changed steady-state condition as:

$$\frac{\lambda}{s} = \frac{y^*}{k^*} = \frac{1}{V^*} \qquad\qquad 2.16$$

and

$$\frac{\lambda}{s_1} = \frac{y^*_1}{k^*_1} = \frac{1}{V^*_1}$$

where

$$\frac{1}{V^*_1} < \frac{1}{V^*}$$

To say that an increase in the savings rate does not affect the equilibrium growth rate of the economy, does not then imply that the level at which the economy is progressing steadily has not been altered. Comparing two economies with identical growth rates, but differing only with regard to their savings ratios, we will find that the one with the higher ratio will have a higher ratio of capital to output. Their higher savings ratio means the employment of more capital per unit of labor and results in a higher level of (y). So that while a change in the savings ratio affects the level of the path along which the growth rate is occuring, it does not affect that rate. Figure (2.4) shows this directly.

Fig. 2.4

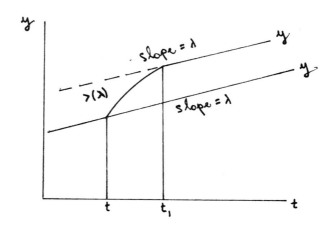

The period between t and t_1 is that transitory phase where
output and capital growth rates exceed (λ).

A further characteristic of an economy in its equilibrium
growth condition is a determined distribution of income. We need
to go back to figure (1.9) in chapter 1 to recall that the rate
of profit is given by the slope of the output per unit of
labor function at the particular level of capital intensity (k^*).
Repeating the outcome here:

$$r = \frac{dY}{dK} \quad f'(k) \qquad\qquad 2.17$$

and

$$k^* \cdot r = \frac{rK}{L}$$

with the difference between (y^*) and $\frac{rK}{L}$ being equal to wages per unit of labor.

Figure (2.5) shows the difference in the distribution
of income associated with the different steady-state conditions.

Fig. 2.5

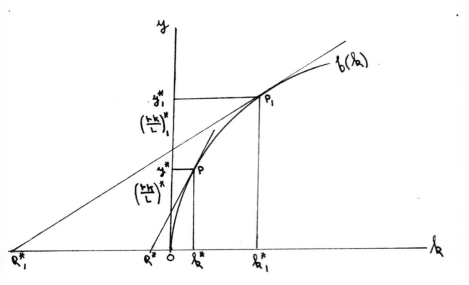

At equilibrium condition (y*), the rate of profit is given by
the tangent at (P) with wages per man being the difference
between Oy* and $(\frac{rK*}{L})$; this constant ratio of wages to profits

is given by the distance OR*. The rate of profit in the steady-
state associated with the higher capital to labor ratio (k_1*)
is shown by the slope of the tangent at (P_1). It is clear that
the more capital intensive state carries with it a lower rate of

profit - as it does a higher wage rate. This higher ratio of wages to profits is seen by the greater distance OR^*_1 reflecting the flatter slope to the tangency at (P_1).

To generalize, we can say that in a comparison of two steady-state conditions we will see an inverse relation between the rate of profit and the state associated with a higher ratio of capital to labor. Or, to put this another way, we see an association between a lower rate of profit and a higher ratio of capital per man to net output per man.

In the transition between y^* and y^*_1, the fact of a higher (k) results initially in a decline in the ratio of capital to output, and thereby an increase in profits per man. The use of capital deepening techniques are associated with an increase in the ratio of profits to wages. But over time, as we discussed, this eventually gives rise to diminishing returns and a decline in the marginal productivity of capital; which prompts the use of techniques that slow the growth of output and hence the growth of the capital stock itself. And this development corresponds to a decline in the ratio of profits to wages. Thus the change in the rate of profit mirrors the change in the techniques of production (the k) as the economy adjusts to the steady-state condition. The slope of a "wage curve" at a point (giving the ratio of the wage rate to the rate of profit) reflects the ratio of the respective marginal productivities and therefore the particular technique in use. We are then able, it seems, to relate the ownership of capital as a means of commanding a share of output, to the productivity of that capital in producting the output.

We put these thoughts together in the following way:

    i. $y = f(k)$

   ii. $r = f'(k)$

  iii. $w = f(k) - kf'(k)$

   iv. $\dfrac{dw}{dk} = -kf''(k) > 0$

               as

       $f''(k) < 0$

    v. $\dfrac{dr}{dk} = f''(k) < 0$

   vi. $\dfrac{\frac{dw}{dk}}{\frac{dr}{dk}} = \dfrac{dw}{dr} = -k$ 2.18

       the ratio of a proportionate change in the wage rate to the rate of profit is:

  vii. $\dfrac{\frac{dw}{w}}{\frac{dr}{r}} = \dfrac{dw}{dr} \cdot -\dfrac{r}{w}$

 viii. and $\dfrac{dw}{dr} = -k$

       so that the elasticity of the wage curve is the ratio of aggregate shares:

       $-\dfrac{r}{w}(-k)$

       or

   ix. $\dfrac{r}{w} \cdot \dfrac{K}{L} = \dfrac{rK}{wL}$

One can read from the wage curve a direct relation between the factor price ratio, the factor input ratio (technique of production) and relative shares.[3]

    Summarizing to this point, we find the neo-classical model portraying an economy that tends towards, and eventually settles into, a state of growth in which the growth rates of the capital stock and output are equal to that of the labor force; and it is drawn to this condition from whatever the initial capital labor ratio happens to be. A hallmark of this equilibrium state is

the choice of technique of production that produces a rate
of growth of the labor force (and thereby, as well as determining a particular ratio of profits to wages.) Attempts to
cause output to grow at a faster rate than that of the labor
force will prove transitorilly successful. We stress again
that while such a move will propel the economy (via a higher
savings rate) to a higher level of output, the growth rate
of that output will be drawn once more to that of the labor
force.

At the beginning of this chapter we asked whether this
neo-classical model can teach us anything about what is really
going on. Now having seen it in operation, we should inquire
as to what kind of reality exists out there. What are the
"stylized facts" (i.e. essentially valid observations) of
economic growth? What are the long run relations between
the growth of labor, capital and output; and between the
inouts of capital and labor and relative income shares?
It has been proposed by Professor Kaldor[4] that a historical
view of the development of capilistic economies shows
evidence that:

i.   The ratio of investment to output remains
      constant.

ii.   The capital to output ratio remains constant.

iii. The rate of profit is fairly constant in the
      long run.

iv.   The capital to labor and output to labor
      ratios are rising.

v.   The real wage is rising.

vi.   The relative share of capital and labor, or the
      ratio of property income to total income remains
      constant. That is, a constant long-run
      relative distribution of output between
      wages and profits.[5]

There is a general agreement concerning these long run observations; so that a model purporting to describe the evolution of developed economies would need to be in harmony with the above properties.

It seems that our model serves well as a parable, except for the fact that while capital and output both grown at the same rate, it is at a faster rate than that of the work force. We need to reconcile the constancy of income shares with the growing capital to labor ratio. This inconsistancy can be corrected by introducing technological change as a factor in the production function. We consider this in the appendix to this chapter.

NOTES

1. Based on the models of R. M. Salow "A Contribution to the Theory
   of Economic Growth," <u>Quarterly Journal of Economics</u>, February 1956,
   pp. 65-94; and that of T. W. Swan, "Economic Growth and Capital
   Accumulation," <u>Economic Record</u>, November 1956, pp. 334-361. Also
   see the discussion in Edwin Burmeister and A. Rodney Dobell,
   <u>Mathematical Theories of Economic Growth</u>, MacMillan, New York
   1970, Chapter 2.

2. We utilize several diagrams found in the explanation by W. H.
   Bronson, <u>Macroeconomic Theory and Policy</u>, Harper and Row,
   New York 1972, Chapter 19.

3. From (iv) we see that the wage-rate varies directly with (k), and
   (v) shows the rate of profit varying inversely with (k). These
   relations are brought together on a wage-curve depicting the
   inverse relation between the wage rate and the rate of profit.

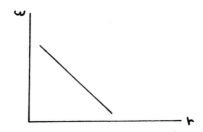

4. N. Kaldor, "Capital Accumulation and Economic Growth" in <u>The
   Theory of Capital</u>, F. A. Lutz and D. C. Hague, MacMillan,
   London 1964.

5. There has been some work of late suggesting that (based in U.S.
   data from 1948-73), labor's relative share has increased while
   capital's relative share has decreased. See W. A. Magat, "Technological Advance with Depletion of Innovation Possibilities –
   Implications for the Dynamics of Factor Shares," <u>Economic Journal</u>,
   September 1979, pp. 614-623.

APPENDIX: THE MODEL WITH TECHNOLOGICAL CHANGE

Before getting into this, let us review certain ideas
that were discussed in Chapter 1. Recall that we characterized
neutral technoligcal change as a condition in which increased
productive capability results from a given input factor
ratio, due to the fact that the productivity of labor and
capital have increased to the same degree. In other words,
we have a change that leaves unchanged the marginal rate of
technical substitution between the factors.
Handling this, via the Cobb-Douglas, we repeat equation (1.39)
of chaper 1:

$$y = Ae^{nt} f(k) \qquad\qquad A.1$$

where the (A) term is that index of technical change showing
the upward shift in output at a rate (n) for a given input
ratio.

The diagramatic representation of this was seen in
figure (1.9) where the distance (OR) indicated the constant
ratio of profits to wages as the production function shifts
upwards. This idea of an equi-proportionate rise in the
productivity of both inputs can be designated as "disembodied
neutral progress". One can picture this as a kind of advance
that falls costlessly per unit of time on the economy
(like manna from heaven) and distributes itself evenly on all
labor and all of capital. We have a situation as if the factors
of production were increasing; effective labor and effective
capital are increasing even though actual labor and actual
capital are constant. Relating this neutral progress to the
steady-state outcome in figure (2.2), would have us shift
upwards the per capita output function by the amount (n).

51

Fig. A.1

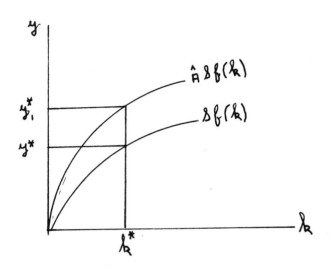

Recalculating output growth, we have:

$$\hat{Y} = \hat{A} + \alpha\hat{K} + (1-\alpha)\,\hat{L} \qquad \text{A.2}$$
$$\hat{A} = \hat{Y} - \alpha\hat{K} - (1-\alpha)\,\hat{L} = n$$

The rate of growth of output at a point in time exceeds the identical growth rates of capital and labor multiplied by their respective output elasticities by a residual equal to the growth rate of (A). The growth of (A) translates into (α) and (1-α) both growing at the (n) rate.

Yet this disembodied technical change does not resolve

the inconsistency of the model. While it does explain the
constant income shares and the rising output to actual labor
ratio (though we have a constant output to effective labor
and capital ratios) it does so within the confines of a constant
value of the ratio of actual capital to actual labor.

Let us now reckon that technical change shows up in the
form of an increase in the productivity of labor at a rate
exogenously determined. And this improvement in the skill of
labor is absorbed equally by all of the labor force; those
already employed with existing capital and those coming into
employment with newly accumulated capital. This labor
augmenting change can be referred to as "embodied" in that it
is calculated via its effect on a particular input (instead
of residing neutrally in all inputs). But the change is
itself "neutral" with regard to the factor in which it
resides; new labor is as productive as old labor. Perhaps one
can refer to this happening as neutral labor-embodied
technical progress.

But regardless of the label, we have one man being
able to do what two men did previously; and therefore an
"as if" growth in the labor force (effective labor increases).
Labor is not only measured in the number of hands, but also in
terms of each pair of hands representing an efficiency unit.
This technical change is proceeding at a rate (n), hence:
$$A = e^{nt} \qquad \text{A.3}$$
And in the production function:
$$Y = F(K, e^{nt}L) \qquad \text{A.4}$$

As time goes on, a given labor force in natural or
nominal units represents an increasing number of efficiency
units because of technical progress. The production function
will shift in conjunction with this increase in labor productivity.

53

But we must also bear in mind that along with this, in terms of natural units, the labor force is also growing at the (λ) rate.

In the model without technical progress, the steady-state growth rate is shown to be equal to that of the growth of the labor force; now with this labor embodied technical progress, it will be shown to be equal to the combined rates of growth of the labor force and technical progress ($\lambda+n$); or, "effective labor" is $L_E = L_0 e^{(\lambda+n)t}$. Let us see how this works out.

We restate the production function on a per unit "effective labor" basis.

i. $y = \dfrac{Y}{L_0 e^{(n+\lambda)t}} = f(\dfrac{K}{L_E}) = f(k)$ A.5

ii. $\dfrac{\dot{k}}{k} \equiv \hat{k} = \hat{K} - \hat{L}_E$

iii. then $\hat{k} = \dfrac{sy}{k} - (n + \lambda)$

iv.   and $\hat{k} = \dfrac{sf(k)}{k} - (n + \lambda)$

The equilibrium condition $\hat{k} = 0$ is now:

i. $\dfrac{sf(k)}{k} = (n + \lambda)$ A.6

or

ii. $sf(k) = (n + \lambda)K$

iii. then $y^* = f(k^*) = \dfrac{n+\lambda}{s} (k^*)$

as compared to the condition in the absence of technical change:

$$y^* = f(k^*) = \dfrac{\lambda}{s} (k^*) \qquad A.7$$

We see this steady-state outcome in figure (A.2)

Fig. A.2

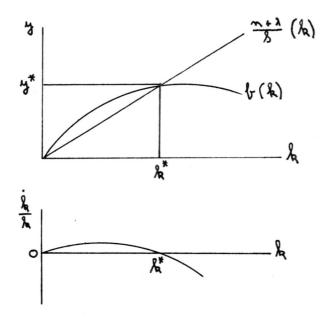

y* is now greater than y* in the absence of technical change since the (n) factor enters into the production function as an "as if" increase in the labor force. The increase in the ratio of capital per natural unit of labor causes output to grow at a rate equal to that of capital itself. Both capital and labor exceed the growth of the labor force in natural terms by the rate of growth of labor in efficiency units. Any tendency to diminishing returns due to capital being accumulated in excess of the growth of labor is offset by the increase in the productivity of labor at the (n) rate. Thus we maintain the ratios.

$$\frac{K}{L_E} = \frac{Y}{L_E} \qquad\qquad A.8$$

in the face of $\dfrac{K}{L_o e^{\lambda t}} > 1$

In summary: both (Y) and (K) grow at the $(n + \lambda)$ rate, while (L) grows at rate (λ), then (y) and (k) both grow at the (n) rate. This is in keeping with the stylized facts which, to reiterate, show both output and capital growing at an identical rate which is greater than the growth of the labor force. Relating to the Cobb-Douglas function, we recognize the common growth rate of output, capital and labor via the proper definition of the growth of labor.
Thus:

$$Y = K^{\alpha}\, L_E^{1-\alpha} \qquad\qquad A.9$$

then $\quad Y = K^{\alpha}\, (L_o e^{\lambda t} e^{nt})^{1-\alpha}$

and $\quad Y = e^{(nt)\,(1-\alpha)}\, [K^{\alpha} L_o e^{(\lambda t)\,(1-\alpha)}]$

The function shifts upward, reflecting the increase in the productivity of labor at the (n) rate.

Next we look at the relative shares of labor and capital with technical progress. The marginal product of capital is now:

$$\frac{dY}{dK} = L_E f'(\frac{k}{L_E}) \cdot \frac{1}{L_E} = f'(k) = r \qquad A.10$$

the rate of profit being equal to the slope of the production function at point k* in figure (A.2)

On the other hand, the wage rate will be rising to reflect the increase in the productivity per unit of natural labor. Thus:

$$w = \frac{dY}{dL} = e^{nt}\, [f(k) - kf'(k)] \qquad A.11$$

The steady-state condition being characterized by a
constant capital to output ratio, will also reveal a constancy
in the ratio of profits to output. The existence of a
growing capital per unit of natural labor ratio results as a
rate of output growth equal to that of capital; and at the
given rate of profit this assures the constancy of capital's
share in output.

With regard to labor's share, we see that the increase
in the productivity of the growing labor force results in a
rate of growth of output equal to that of effective labor,
with wages growing at a rate $(\lambda+n)$. Thus we maintain the
constancy in the ratio of wages to output, and hence in
the ratio of capital's share to that of labor, in the
face of both capital and output exceeding the growth of
the labor force.

Let us set out this result in the following way. The
capital to (natural) labor ratio is rising at the (n) rate:

$$ke^{nt} \qquad\qquad A.12$$

and the rate of the rate of profit to the wage rate is:

$$\frac{r}{W} = \frac{f'(k)}{e^{nt}\,[f(k) - kf'(k)]} \qquad A.13$$

Relating (A.12) and (A.13) gives in the ratio of profits to
wages when capital is growing at a rate equal to the growth
of labor in efficiency units. Thus:

$$\frac{f'(k)}{e^{nt}\,[f(k) - kf'(k)]} \cdot ke^{nt} \qquad A.14$$

and

$$\frac{r}{w}\,(k) \equiv \frac{rK}{rL}$$

showing relative income shares constant at the equilibrium capital

57

to effective labor ratio.

This technical change that we have been discussing is
referred to as Harrod-neutral. It indicates a constancy in
the ratio of profits to wages along a growth path characterized
by a constant capital to output ratio. Putting this another
way, we can state that this type neutrality prevails if a
shift of the production function resulting in an increase in
the capital to natural unit labor ratio, leaves the rate of
profit unchanged. Consider figure (A.3).

Fig. A.3

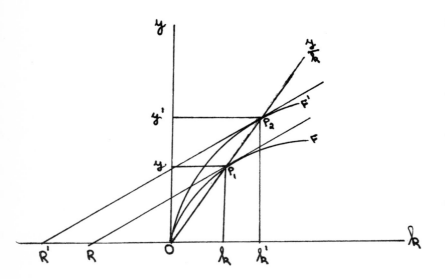

Output and capital per head are in terms of natural units.
The shift of the production function showing an increase in
capital per head leaves unchaged the output to capital ratio,

as P_1 and P_2 are on the same radius from the origin. The constant marginal product of capital is seen from the parallel slopes of the tangents at P_1 and P_2; with the unchanged rates of income shares shown by the parallel intersections at R and R'.

To this one can juxtapose the neutral technical progress discussed earlier in the appendix, and referred to as Hicks-neutral. The essential point of this approach is that it describes a situation where the ratio of profits to wages is unchanged along a path that evidences a constant rate of capital to natural unit of labor.

With the inclusion of labor-augmenting technical change our neoclassical model seems to have emerged as a suitable vehicle to explain the stylized facts of economic growth. Or has it? Do we feel any discomfort with its basic construction?

3. A QUESTION OF CAPITAL AND THE PRODUCTION FUNCTION
I

We place a quantity of something called capital into a production function to explain the flow of output; and we take the marginal product of this capital in response to changes in its quantity per capita to determine or explain the rate of profit, and thus the level of profits per capita. In order to have done this, we had to homogenize the reality of the heterogeneous nature of capital into a uniform metaphorical device, and endow it with the capability to embody various techniques of production (to adopt to different capital/labor ratios) without losing its identifiable physical quantity.

With regard to the labor input, one can treat all labor alike and identify the change in the quantity of this input in terms of man-hours of labor. But in what unit is capital to be measured? Is there a way to aggregate the diveristy of sizes, shapes and specifications of the units that comprise what capital is into a common unit of measurement? Or must we, in order to treat this input, fall back on the fantasy of a quantity of ectoplasm or lump of leets.

Note that in boiling down the diversity of capital into such a composite fantasy unit, one is able to recognize and measure different quantities of the "capital" in a physical sense, and hence apart from a value of capital notion, and the rate of profit which enters into a determination of this value. Indeed, one must be able to measure a quantity of capital this way if we are to hold that is is the marginal product of capital that determines what the rate of profit is. Holding to this means that we can make compatible the treatment of capital as a productive instrument with the

treatment of it as an instrument in determining the distribution of income. Otherwise, we are faced with a situation that
the marginal product of capital as a determinant of the rate
of profit is itself indeterminate in the absence of knowing
what the rate of profit is.

Consider that the aggregation of capital into a common
value index can be done by obtaining its present value through
the future flow of earnings, or by a value based on the past
costs incurred in its production. Taking the former approach,
suppose we have a piece of capital that is expected to yield
a stream of future net earnings of $100 in each of four years,
after which it ceases to be productive. The present value of
this capital is the sum of the discounted flow of this future
profit. Given a rate of interest (a rate of profit) of 4%
we have: 3.1

$$\text{Present Value} = \frac{100}{1.04} + \frac{100}{(1.04)^2} + \frac{100}{(1.04)^3} + \frac{100}{(1.04)^4} = 363.49$$

Valuing all capital in this manner gives us an index of
the stock of capital in terms of value. But to do this, one
has to say something about the profit stream, which means
estimating future prices and costs; and then, given a rate
of interest we can value the capital good. Thus the recog-
nition of an "amount" of capital in the production function
requires that the interest rate be known beforehand.

The whole notion of forming a value index (let us say a
value composit) of a large variety of capital goods and
constructing a production function, and then taking a measure
of its slope to determine the rate of profit, involves
circularity of reasoning. What is needed is to find a non-
fantasy unit in which capital may be aggregated and measured as
a physical number so that we can feel comfortable about

61

coupling it with a likewise numerical expression for the labor input.

We can get at this by following our second approach and valuing capital in terms of its past costs of production; and then going behind this money veil, to relate to real units of production. To quote Joan Robinson, "Clearly money cost of production is neither here nor there unless we can specify the purchasing power of money, but we may cost the capital good in terms of wage units, that is in effect to measure their cost in terms of a unit of standard labor."[1] Her proposal is to value capital in terms of the quantity of labor time expended in its production. One should recognize the act of investment as the employment of labor now in such a way as to yield the fruit of this employment in the future. The labor time of the past is carried forward to be used again at a later date, because this past labor comes to us in the form of capital. In other words, capital is that good which allows past labor to make current labor more productive.

But looking at capital this way still does not avoid the basic problem of finding a physical measure of capital without first having to consider a rate of profit. For the value of capital to be reckoned in terms of labor time never comes to us composed solely of labor time. Past labor embodied in today's capital must itself be thought of as having worked with existing capital or with natural resources (if one conceives of going back to the beginning of matters.) As Mrs. Robinson so aptly points out, "When Adam delved and Eve span there were evidently a spade and a spindle already in existence."[2] In a production function today's labor is being added to the product of past labor which, in its own time, was added to the product of still earlier labor and so on.

62

Consider that firm (X) undertakes an investment project whereby it purchases labor and also materials and ready-made equipment from firm (Y). For these purchases, (X) pays a price which includes an allowance for a profit at the ruling rate of profit. To these labor and capital costs firm (X) will add a profit charge which is reckoned as a notional cost of this investment and which is to be covered by the value of it. Thus the total cost of the investment exceeds the sum of the actual outlays by the rate of profit, as did cost exceed outlay one step before on the part of firm (Y). What we come to is that the value of the capital produced by (X) depends on the rate of profit placed on the outlay by (X), and by (Y) on this outlay (as it determines cost to X) and so on going back in time; and it is this value that is to be measured in labor time. The value of capital at a point in time is the result of the value of previous outlays (previous equipment combined with a given amount of labor) compounded at a particular rate of profit. In other words, the actual value of labor time embodied in a piece of equipment is less than the value of the equipment, and it is this latter value that is measured in labor time.

But then two alike machines produced with the same quantity of man-hours will have different values depending upon the rate of profit under which they have been produced. In a condition of a lower rate of profit the cost of capital is lower, and it is reckoned as such in terms of labor time; while the higher cost machine due to the higher rate of profit is reckoned in terms of a greater amount of labor time. This difference in the value of the machines in spite of their having the same labor hours expended in their production tells us something important. The higher value of capital

63

tells us that it is a resource that is more scarce relative
to labor. The production of an output that is relatively
scarce represents a large investment in real terms (labor hours)
as compared with the production of a relatively abundant good.

We must also note that two pieces of equipment may have
different values at the same rate of profit. The difference
being attributable to the amount of real labor time (degree of
roundaboutness) embodied in its production. The greater the
length of the "average period of production," the greater the
value. We seem to have a measure of capital that is independent
of distribution, ie. that a change in its value can be taken
independent of a change in the rate of profit.

II

Now we can get at Joan Robinson's notion of the capital/
labor ratio. She uses the term real capital ratio, which is
a ratio of capital in terms of past labor compounded at a
given profit rate to the amount of labor currently employed
when it is working at normal capacity. To reiterate, it is
not the same labor time in both elements of the ratio. The
denominator consists of a flow per unit of time of current
labor, while the numerator consists of past labor time
currently employed via its embodyment in the capital stock;
where the total of this labor results from past labor being, so
to speak, cumulatively increased at the rate of profit.

This implies we draw a separate output per capita
curve as a function of the variation in the capital/labor
ratio for each level of the rate of profit. Each point on the
curve has got to be considered with regard to the quantity
of past labor time resulting from a change in the actual number
of machines and not from a change in their value (as reflected
in the profit rate). in addition, it is necessary that the

64

different stocks of capital represent different quantities
of alike equipment; for the productivity per unit of labor may
change due to a change in the "roundabout" nature of the
equipment that go to make up the different quantities of past
labor time per capita. In general, the productivity curve
has got to be drawn for a given rate of profit, and must
be related to different quantities of exact replicas of a
previous capital stock.

In drawing up a production function we would then have to
reckon each point on the function as reflective of a steady-
state condition; one in which a given rate of profit exists
and is expected to rule in the future, and in which a stock
of capital of a particular productive capacity is being employed.
If we look back to figure (2.1) in chapter 2, the move from
one level of the capital intensity ratio to another has got to
be handled in terms of the fantasy unit; or if not, that it
encompasses a time span short enough as not to allow a change
in the capacity of the units comprising the changed quantity
of the non-fantasy capital stock. But such a time span
cannot be real (we have to assume that the stock of capital
does not change, or that if it is changing, it is not an
exact replica of previous capital that is being accumulated).
We cannot treat the production function as a curve upon
which one moves from point to point to an equilibrium position;
and the Robinsonian function which we will look at does not.

We develop the conditions for the existance of a
particular technique in the steady-state. Consider:

K – capital stock in terms of output
w – wage rate in terms of output
r – rate of profit
L_K– labor need to produce a unit of capital t periods ago
L_c– current labor employed

The value of equipment can then be reckoned in past labor time, but it includes an allowance for profit on the costs incurred in the past to create the stock of capital today. Hence, as we discussed, this value must be expressed as a function of the rate of profit. We can write:

$$K = wL_K (1 + r)^t \qquad\qquad 3.2$$

and capital in terms of labor time (K_L):

$$K_L = \frac{K}{w} = L_K (1 + r)^t \qquad\qquad 3.3$$

Given the same quantity of man-hours (L_K), capital in terms of labor time is an increasing function of the rate of profit.

In equilibrium we have an unchanging rate of profit, and all existing equipment are earning profits at this rate. One piece of capital (representing the use of a particular technique) will differ in cost from another (representing the use of another technique) by virtue of the difference in past labor time involved, and not by the virtue of earning profit at a higher rate. Presume three techniques α, β, and γ listed in descending order with regard to output per head when coupled with labor working at normal capacity. Again we want to stress that the alpha technique is termed more mechanized than beta because it involves a greater quantity of capital (in terms of past labor time invested) per unit of current labor employed.

For a given wage rate the firm chooses that technique of production – out of a hierarchy of techniques each costed at the given rate of profit – that will yield the greatest surplus over wage cost so as to obtain the highest rate of profit. Let us consider the following example.

Table 3.1

Technique	α	β	γ
Wage Rate	1	1	1
Cost of Technique	100	50	25
Product	65	60	55
Wage Bill	50	50	50
Profit	15	10	5
Rate of Profit	15%	20%	20%

The techniques are ordered according to the rate of output produced with a given number of mean, each technique is utilized with 50 men. The entries are expressed in physical units in terms of the firm's own product. We see that the technique with the higher rate of output requires a larger investment per man. Note that technique (α) does not compensate for the higher cost of this technique with the result that (α) earns the lowest rate of profit. At the particular wage rate of 1 per man techniques (β) and (γ) are indifferent.

Now assume that the ruling wage is 1.1, and the cost of the techniques increase to reflect this 10% change.

Table 3.2

Technique	α	β	γ
Wage Rate	1.1	1.1	1.1
Cost of Technique	110	55	27.5
Product	65	60	55
Wage Bill	55	55	55
Profit	10	5	0
Rate of Profit	9%	9%	0

At this higher wage rate techniques (α) and (β) are indifferent and (γ) is out of the running.

For each of the existing techniques the value of output is:

$$Y = wL_c + rwL_K (1 + r)^t \qquad\qquad 3.4$$

[for technique (α) at wage rate 1 output
is $65 = 1(50) + .15 (100)$].

$$\text{then:} \quad w = \frac{Y}{L_c + rL_K(1+r)^t} \qquad\qquad 3.5$$

Given the wage rate, one finds the technique (or set of
techniques) that yields the highest rate of profit. At wage
rate 1 (which may be called the β-γ rate) all labor may be
employed with β or with γ or with a combination of the two.
But then we can presume a wage rate above β-γ at which β
is the most profitable (at rate 1.07); we can ascend a series
of wage rates to a point of a β-α rate (that of 1.10), and
then on to a rate of 1.12 at which technique α is brought
into play. The point is, that as wage rates increase the
system responds by adopting techniques that have a higher real
capital ratio and produce a higher ratio of output per man.

We can now go on to draw the Robinsonian production
function relating the rate of output per period of time on
the verticle axis to the real capital ratio on the horizontal.
Since the amount of labor currently employed is constant the
verticle axis does not represent output per man-year (the 55
output is equivalent to 1.1 man-years). As we will see,
points on this function are to be regarded as steady-state
or equilibrium positions.

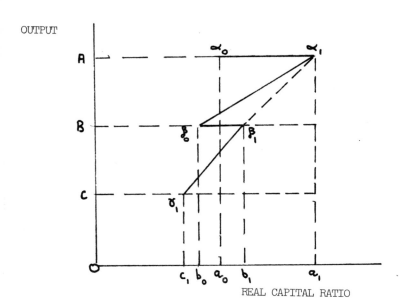

Fig. 3.1

OA, OB and OC are the rates of output in descending order for the three techniques α, β and γ. Points a_1, b_1 and c_1 show the real capital ratio corresponding to each of the techniques as they are costed at the same rate of profit. As we descend from α to γ we have lower rates of output associated with lower real capital ratios. Then for a given rate of profit one can draw a productivity curve, α_1, β_1, γ_1; and consider this curve as reflective of table 3.1 where β and γ are equally profitable. Let us assume that all labor is employed with the gamma technique, so that we have a point on the production function relating the rate of output to the real capital ratio (all expressed in labor units)

69

for the given wage rate 1.

For a prevailing higher wage rate the factor ratio in use would be Ob_1, and all labor would be employed with the beta technique. But we are now in a different equilibrium position; the higher wage rate (at 1.07) means a lower ruling rate of profit by which the capital outfits (techniques) would have been costed. Thus the move from γ_1 to β_1 involves a horizontal jump from β_1 to β_0 corresponding to the lower rate of profit when the wage rate is such as to have us adopt the beta technique. The real capital ratio increases from Oc_1 to Ob_0. For the higher wage rate the system selects a technique that maximizes the rate of profit, with the value of capital in terms of past labor time now compunded at this ruling lower rate of profit. We see the result of the wage rate at 1.07 in table 3.3.

Table 3.3

Technique	α	β	γ
Wage Rate	1.07	1.07	1.07
Cost of Technique	107	53.50	26.75
Product	65	60	55
Wage Bill	53.50	53.50	53.50
Profit	11.50	6.50	1.50
Rate of Profit	10%	12%	.05%

For a still higher wage rate where α_1 would be called into being, we take another horizontal jump to α_0, to a productivity curve reflective of a still lower rate of profit. The real capital ratio increases from b_0 to a_0. The production function consists of points γ_1, β_0 and α_0 corresponding to real capital ratios c_1, b_0 and a_0.

In the Robinsonian function we have to be given the rate of profit as separate information along with the technology in order to determine the factor ratio (and hence income distribution) and

70

the rate of output. Whereas in the traditional function it is the marginal product of the factor in response to a change in its quantity that determines its earnings; one deduces income shares from the productivity curve. But now we understand that to take this latter approach one must over-look specifying the units of measurement, i.e. one aggregates the diversity of capital into homogeneous fantasy units. Otherwise, one cannot go from the productivity curve to a relation between wages and profits, since the curve cannot be specified without knowing before hand what the rate of profit is.

Mrs. Robinson's design was not to abandon the production function, but as she puts it, "to rescue the element of common sense that has been entangled in it."[3] That is, that capital is a productive agent, and that different profit levels will be associated with different quantities of this agent and different output rates. Furthermore, one can compare two systems with different existing stocks of capital associated with different wage rates, and say something about the differing shares of output. What a production function can do is to provide a means for a comparitive analysis. What it cannot do is to provide a way to see how the system gets into an equilibroum position; we must, it seems, not depart from a comparison of stationary states.

And yet, a production function constructed by reducing the diversity of capital into some kind of uniform capital good, was the medium to explain those stylized facts of economic development. Are we then to say that if capital cannot be aggregated into a measure that is independent of income distribution, and that if we also do not want to escape into fantasy, that our conclusions drawn from the neo-classical

71

model are invalid? Clearly not. Facts remain facts, even
if the mechanism used to explain them is fantasy. This leads
to the question as to whether there is any situation in which
the reality of heterogeneous capital goods will yield the
same outcome as generated by the neo-classical "fairy tale",
thus making the medium as real as the message. In part III
we turn to this possibility.

III

Professor Samuelson, in a paper entitled "Parable and
Realism in Capital Theory: The Surrogate Production Function"
demonstrates that the properties (at least with regard to
distribution) emanating from the traditional production
function can also be generated from a world characterized
by heterogeneous capital goods and fixed input proportions.
In Samuelson's words, "What I propose to do here is to show
that a new concept, 'the surrogate production function,'
can provide some rationalization for the validity of the
simple J. B. Clark parables which pretend there is a single
thing called 'capital' that can be put into a single
production function and along with labor will produce total
output."[4] But as we shall see, Professor Samuelson's argument
rests on a somewhat special assumption. Let us first be
certain as to what this fixed (L-shaped) production function
is all about. A fixed input coefficient technology means
that production of a unit of output requires the being of a
particular ratio of capital to labor. This function is written as:

$$Y = \min \left[\frac{1}{a_K} (K), \frac{1}{a_L} (L)\right] \qquad 3.6$$

where a_K, a_L are the required minimum inputs of capital and labor.
Full employment of capital, for example, presumes that for a
given level of output, the amount of capital employed is equal
to that level of output multiplied by the minimum capital input

per unit of output; and this is equal to the available
capital. Then, for both capital and labor, we have:

$$K = a_K Y \qquad\qquad 3.7$$

$$L = a_L Y \qquad\qquad 3.8$$

and

$$\frac{K}{Y} = a_K, \ \frac{L}{Y} = a_L, \ \frac{K}{L} = \frac{a_K}{a_L} \qquad\qquad 3.9$$

In figure (3.2) we see such an L-shape function with slope
$\frac{a_K}{a_L}$, locating it for output levels 1 and 2.

Fig. 3.2

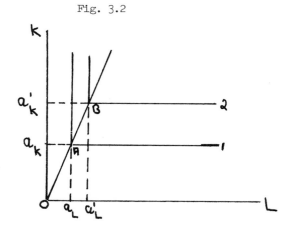

Using this technique with greater intensity (increasing production) requires that capital and labor grow in such a manner
as to always present the necessary ratio between them; a

doubling of output requires a doubling of input (there are no economies or diseconomies in the use of the technique). Should the ratio fall below $\frac{a_K}{a_L}$, there will be unemployed labor. The resulting change in the ratio of input prices can have no effect on the proportion of inputs used. In this situation the necessary increase in the capital stock to fully employ the labor force falls short of the actual rate of accumulation; labor is unemployed as:

$$L > Ya_L \qquad\qquad 3.10$$

We can say that the demand for labor is governed by the rate of growth of capital, with the problem being that the demand for labor is insufficient.

Consider the economy having at its disposal a set of techniques or production processes, where each technique is characterized by the L-shaped production function. To reiterate, each technique uses a particular "structure" of capital (working with a fixed amount of labor) that differs from that used with any of the other techniques with regard to the level of output wrought by it. We can say that the capital related to each process differ in their degree of mechanization.

Each of these fixed proportions processes (α, β and γ) can be used to produce consumption goods. This rests on the special assumption that a particular production function, i.e. a particular slope a_K/a_L, is the same in the production of the capital good or consumption good; the ratio of the inputs and their absolute magnitudes are the same for either output thus we relate the production function to output generally as in equation (3.6).

74

We now set out the equations for the rate of profit and the wage rate that accompany the use of a production process. From equation (3.6) we have:

$$Y = \frac{K}{a_K}, \; \frac{L}{a_L} \qquad 3.11$$

and

$$K = \frac{L}{a_L} (a_K) = \frac{a_K}{a_L} (L) \qquad 3.12$$

Profits are $Y - wL$ 3.13

and the rate of profit (r) is

$$r = \frac{Y-wL}{K} = \frac{1}{a_K} - \frac{a_L}{a_K} (w) \qquad 3.14$$

$[$as $\frac{Y}{K} = \frac{1}{a_K}, \; \frac{L}{K} = \frac{a_L}{a_K}]$

also from (3.14)

$$\frac{a_L}{a_K} (w) = \frac{1}{a_K} - r \qquad 3.15$$

and

$$w = \frac{1}{a_L} - \frac{a_K}{a_L} (r) \qquad 3.16$$

Statement (3.16) has been called the wage equation or, as Professor Samuelson refers to it, the factor-price equation.

This wage equation depicts a straight line negative relation between the wage rate and the rate of profit; with the slope of the line being the fixed ratio of capital to labor.

Fig. 3.3

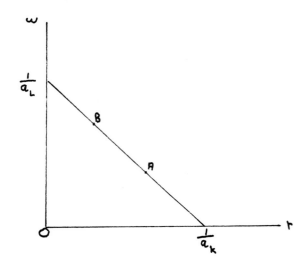

The intercept $1/a_K$ gives the rate of profit when the wage
rate is zero; all income accrues to capital and total profit
is ra_K. Similarly $1/a_L$ gives the maximum wage rate when
capital is a free good, with total wages being wa_L. The wage
rate becomes zero when $ra_K = 1$, so that for the reality of a
wage greater than zero we need that $r < 1/a_K$ and for a positive
rate of profit we need $w < 1/a_L$.

At a given wage the system will adapt the production
process that maximizes the rate of profit. But the choice of a
process is that of a suite or structure of capital goods
that offers a given amount of employment. An assumption of
full-employment means that the existing wage leads to a

76

technique being chosen such that its capital structure
employs the given labor force. Consider the alpha technique
with a particular distribution of income represented by point
(A) in figure (3.3) to be such a condition. Should labor's
share rise by a third in the move to a point (B), then the
share going to capital falls by the same proportion. Within
the frame of a given technique, one cannot react to this
change in shares by altering input proportions; but one can
react by moving to another technique characterized by
different fixed proportions.

There are two pieces of information that can be read
from a given wage curve pertaining to the distribution of
output. We see that the slope of the curve is the aggregate
capital to labor ratio, and secondly that the elasticity of
a change in the ratio of the wage rate to the rate of profit
is the ratio of factor shares. From (3.16) we read the
change in (w) for a change in (r) as:

$$i. \quad \frac{a_K}{a_L} = -\frac{dw}{dr}$$

$$ii. \quad a_K = \frac{K}{Y}, \; a_L = \frac{L}{Y}$$

$$iii. \quad \frac{a_K}{a_L} = \frac{K}{L} \qquad\qquad 3.17$$

$$iv. \quad \frac{\frac{dw}{w}}{\frac{dr}{r}} = -\frac{r}{w} \cdot \frac{dw}{dr}$$

$$v. \quad -\frac{r}{w} \cdot \frac{dw}{dr} = \frac{rK}{wL}$$

Note again that a point on a wage curve (i.e. a technique curve)
shows a ratio of factor shares as given by the elasticity of
the curve at that point. And, for the given income distribution,
the technique that is in use is most profitable. Should the

elasticity be less than unity, then the use of the technique
is accompanied by capital receiving more than half the value
of output.

In figure (3.4) we find the (α) technique in use with
a factor payment ratio at point (A). A reduction in the
wage rate leads to the adoption of a different technique
such as to maximally increase the rate of profit. Whereas
technique alpha was best at wage rate (w), we now find
technique beta at point (B) reflective of the lower rate (w').

Fig. 3.4

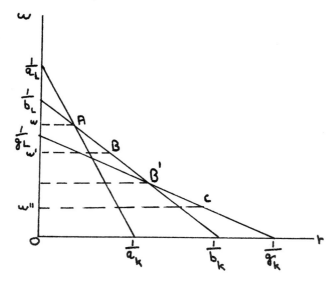

The intercepta of the beta technique curve tell us that the
corresponding maximum rate of profit when w = 0 is $1/b_K > 1/a_K$
(thus $b_K < a_K$); and the maximum real wage when r = 0 is $1/b_L < 1/a_L$

(thus $b_L > a_L$). That is, the slope of the beta curve is
less than that of alpha $(\frac{b_K}{b_L} < \frac{a_K}{a_L})$; we find a decline in the
wage rate associated with the adoption of a technique that in-
volves a lower capital to labor ratio. Given the lower wage
it will, so to speak, pay to put into operation a technique
that is less mechanized, i.e. that employs a greater amount of
labor units. A further fall in the wage rate to (w") will
have the economy adopt the gamma technique at point (C).
Here again we find $g_K < b_K$ and $g_L > b_L$, so that $\frac{g_K}{g_L} < \frac{b_K}{b_L}$;
the still lower wage rate (higher rate of profit) is associated
with a still lower capital to labor ratio. For any given
wage rate it is the technique curve furthest out that yields
the highest rate of profit, and as the wage rate falls, the
economy adjusts to a different outermost curve. This adjustment forms what Professor Samuelson refers to as the "factor-
price frontier" which, in this example, is defined by the
set of three production processes.

The frontier consists of straight line segments such as
$1/a_L$ to A and A to B', on which relative shares can be read
by calculating the elasticity of the factor-price change at
a point on the segment; it also consists of corner (i.e. switch)
points at which two techniques are equi-profitable. Here we
can suppose production to result from a combination of
processes in some proportion, but we will examine switch
points in some detail further along in this work. What we need
to focus on now, is that the frontier curve constructed out of
the three processes evidences similar characteristics to that
of the traditional production function constructed out of the
fantasy homogeneous capital. The factor price frontier can

79

therefore act as a surrogate for the neoclassical production
function, and it does not involve itself with that uniform
malleable capital. We do read from this surrogate function
that the ratio of factor shares is given by the elasticity
of the wage curve at a point, that there is a negative
association between the degree of mechanization (the value of
capital per man) and the rate of profit and that there is
an association between lower rate of profit and higher ratios
of capital to output. The message of the traditional
function derived from the aggregation of capital, is validated
for the real world of heterogeneous capital and fixed proportions. But this confirmations holds only in the special situation
where the absolute level of capital and labor that comprise
the fixed proportion process is alike in all lines of production.

Yet aside from this proviso, we are still left with a
somewhat uneasy feeling. How is capital to be identified
along with this surrogate function? Neoclassicals identify
capital as a physical quantity of an alike substance whose
existence is measurable independent of prices. From this
point of view, we would conceive of a set of physical non-
uniform types of capital; and then, depending on the wage
rate, different capital would be brought into operation from
which one can calculate the physical marginal product, which
is then the rate of profit on that particular piece of
capital. For example, the rate of return to the beta capital
is beta capital over beta capital; in other words, the reality
of the value of a unit production is treated as a fixed amount
pf physical beta capital. This enables the ratio of output
over input to be seen in terms of the same physical quantity.
But it is this mixed up perspective that causes all the
difficulty.

The surrogate does not escape the Robinsonian critique
of the entire marginal productivity approach. At a point
on the function, the process in use earns a rate of profit
on the value of capital which is reckoned on existing
prices corresponding to that rate of profit. We are back to
a circularity of reasoning. The difficulty, it seems comes
from viewing the heterogeneous capital (dollar value) world
as if it were composed of homogeneous physical capital,
and applies to the former conclusions based on the latter.
In chapter 4 we look at a procedure that made it easy to
think this way.

IV

We can appreciate just how restrictive the condition
for the surrogate function outcome, by looking at a similar
two sector fixed proportion model that does not collapse
into an aggregate production function of equation (3.6). We
turn to Professor Hicks' construction in which factor
proportions may be the same in both sectors, but the
absolute magnitudes of the inputs differe in each.[5]

Consider the coefficients a & b, α & β as the inputs
of capital and labor per unit of output of the capital and
consumption sectors respectively; and aslo (w) and (q) as the
wage of labor and earnings of capital respectively. The
sector value equations showing the price of each output being
equal to the direct cost of its production is:

$$\text{capital good} - \rho = aq + bw \qquad 3.18$$

$$\text{consumption good} - \P = \alpha q + \beta w \qquad 3.19$$

Assuming gross and net earnings are the same, then earnings
of capital can be stated as:

$$q = r\rho \qquad 3.20$$

With the rate of profit (r) as:

$$r = \frac{q}{\rho} \qquad 3.21$$

Taking the consumption good as numerator we restate the price equations:

$$\rho = a(r\rho) + bw \qquad 3.22$$

$$1 = \alpha(r\rho) + \beta w \qquad 3.23$$

With the technique of production chracterized by equi-proportionality of inputs in the two sectors, we have:

$$a/b = \alpha/\beta \qquad 3.24$$

Or, stated in terms of the ratio of capital to labor coefficients (m):

$$m = \frac{a\beta}{b\alpha} = 1 \qquad 3.25$$

Given the full-employment of capital and labor, then:

$$K = K(a) + C(\alpha) \qquad 3.26$$

$$L = K(b) + C(\beta)$$

K — machine (capital) sector
C — consumption good sector

and

$$\frac{K}{Y} = a + \alpha, \ \frac{L}{Y} = b + \beta, \ \frac{K}{L} = \frac{a+\alpha}{b+\beta} \qquad 3.27$$

Though the capital stock can be used as input for the production of a unit capital good and a unit consumption good, the co-efficients will differ and must sum to the existing capital. This is different from the Samuelson story in which the existing capital stock equals the capital coefficient for a unit output in either sector. One would suppose that (a) equal to (α) and (b) equal to (β); but if this were the case, we would find that the ratio (α/β) which in Hicks' interpretation defines the slope of the wage curve, would equal that of the aggregate capital to labor ratio and we come up with the surrogate function result. But this is not the case.

We now work up the wage curve. Dividing equation (3.23) by (w):

$$\frac{1}{w} = \frac{r\rho}{w}(\alpha) + \beta \qquad\qquad 3.28$$

and from (3.22) $\rho(1-ar) = bw$ $\qquad\qquad 3.29$

then $\dfrac{\rho}{w} = \dfrac{b}{1-ar}$ $\qquad\qquad 3.30$

and

$$\frac{1}{w} = r(\frac{b}{1-ar})\ \alpha + \beta$$

$$= \frac{rb\alpha + \beta - \beta ar}{1-ar} \qquad\qquad 3.31$$

so that $w = \dfrac{1-ar}{\beta + (b\alpha-\beta a)r}$ $\qquad\qquad 3.32$

When m = 1 (i.e. $b\alpha = \beta a$) the wage equation reads:

$$w = \frac{1-ar}{\beta}$$

$$= \frac{1}{\beta} - \frac{a}{\beta}(r) \qquad\qquad 3.33$$

Note that the slope of the curve simply does not give the aggregate capital to labor ratio; hence the elasticity of the curve cannot say anything about the ratio of aggregate shares. However, what we do have is:

$$\frac{r}{w} \cdot \frac{dw}{dr} = \frac{r\alpha}{w\beta} \qquad\qquad 3.34$$

The elasticity gives us a ratio of profits in the capital sector to wages in the consumption secotr. We can then make no set statement about the relationship between factor price ratio and the aggregate capital/labor ratio.

We see this in figure (3.5).

83

Fig. 3.5

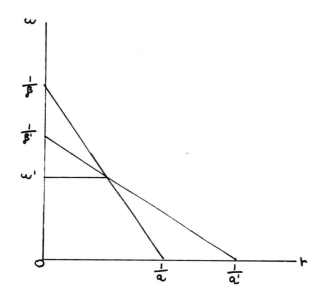

There are techniques A and B, with the intercepts of the A
technique being 1/β and 1/a as derived from the wage equation
(3.34).On the assumption that the technique in play is one
which maximizes the rate of profit for a given real wage,
then there is a switching of techniques on either side (w').
At a wage below w' the switch is to technique B with the
intercepts 1/a' and 1/β'. Thus as wage rates fall, the
system will at some point, switch over to a technique characterized by a lower capital coefficient in the capital goods
sector (a'<a) and a higher labor coefficient in the consumption goods sector (β'>β). But nothing can be said from the

84

wage curve about the labor/output ratio in the capital sector
nor about the capital/output ratio in the consumption sector.

This outcome also holds if m≠1. Should m<1, then the
absolute difference in the magnitudes of the coefficients
relates to the capital sector having the greater ratio of
capital to labor; that is, a/b>α/β. The wage curves show
up as concave from below as seen in figure (3.6).

Fig. 3.6

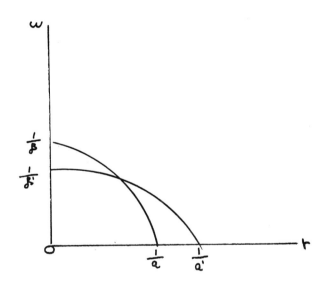

And when m>1 (a/b<α/β) the curves are concave from above as in
figure (3.7).

Fig. 3.7

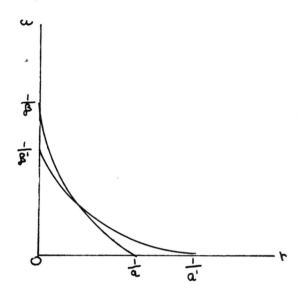

It appears that we cannot fall back on a neoclassical
production function to construct the steady-state conditons and
to reveal its characteristics; for example, that an equilibrium
condition with a high level of wages is associated with a high
capital to labor ratio and a low profit rate, so that income
distribution can be read from a point on the wage curve. A
heterogeneous capital model will, under the reasonable Hicks
assumptions, not yield the results of the traditional function.
Yet even if we suspend disabelief and accept homogeneous

capital, the "normal" results break down in the face of the
Hicks' model; but in accepting this analytical tool we are
engaging in fantasy as a way to dodge the Robinsonian
critique, that it is circular reasoning to talk about a rate
of profit being determined by the slope of a curve depicting
the value of the capital to labor ratio. In general, the
invariant relation between the capital to labor ratio and the
factor price ratio is called into question.

Notes

1. Joan Robinson, "The Production Function and the Theory of Capital." <u>Review of Economic Studies</u>, #55, Vol. XXI, 1953-54.

2. Ibid, p. 82

3. Ibid, p. 83

4. Paul A. Samuelson, "Parable and Realism in Capital Theory: The Surrogate Production Function," in the <u>Collected Papers of P. A. Samuelson</u>, Joseph E. Stiglitz, M.I.T. Press, 1966. p. 324. Originally published in <u>Review of Economic Studies</u>, #XXIX.

5. John Hicks, <u>Capital and Growth</u> Oxford Univeristy Press, N.Y. 1965. In particular chapters 12 and 13.

4. MORE ON CAPITAL AND THE PROFIT RATE

In this chapter we look further at the reasoning underlying the neoclassical production function and the generalizations drawn from it.[1]

Suppose we produce a quantity of a good Y using technique α – current production is Y_α – and that a permanent increase in production can be had by a switchover to a technique β. The payment for implanting this β system is made by an exchange of a quantity of Y_α output $(\overline{Y}_\alpha)$. In effect, the switchover requires us to forego the consumption of a portion of the revenue from the sale of Y_α, and use this savings to purchase the new technique. The reward for this "investment transaction" can be seen in terms of a ratio of the increase in production to the cost or sacrifice of moving to β. Thus:

$$ r = \frac{Y_\beta - Y_\alpha}{Y_\alpha - \overline{Y}_\alpha} \qquad 4.1 $$

where (r) is the rate of profit associated with an investment that changes the technique of production. The capital goods represented by the denominator is not the output of the numerator; nevertheless, the amount of current production that is to be "transferred" into the needed capital becomes known once the price between them is determined. In this way, the capital input can be represented in terms of the goods in the numerator. But the price of this technique reflects the existence of a particular distribution between profits and wages, i.e. the being of a particular rate of profit. Thus in a world of heterogeneous goods, where the numerator and denominator are composed of different outputs, a ratio such as expression (4.1) cannot be structured independent of an already existing rate of profit. It will be profitable or not to undertake the β project, according as to whether (r) is greater or smaller than an existing rate of profit. It bears repeating that this ratio of different goods is constructed to look as if it were composed of the same good (the homogeneous world) because of the assumption of a ruling set of prices. It is this which permits the capital of the denominator to be expressed in terms of the final output of the numerator.

Now we deal again with ratio (4.1) in a broader context. There is production using technique α, and the question is whether or not to switch over to technique β; and in order to accomplish this change, the system needs to add an additional amount of capital to the stock that goes to make up the α technique. But suppose that some of the capital used in the α arrangement becomes superfluous in the β arrangement (consider this as K'_α); i.e. only a part of the existing capital can be joined up with the additional capital that brings in the β productive system. Once more we have a ratio for this change-over as:

$$r = \frac{Y_\beta - Y_\alpha}{K_\beta - [K_\alpha - K'_\alpha]} \qquad 4.2$$

Where the denominator represents the physical quantities to be added to the capital stock. This ratio (4.2) is directly expressed in heterogeneous commodities, so that to reckon the rate of profit, the ratio must be put in value terms. Thus the ratio cannot be taken independent of a particular rate of profit and an accompanying set of prices; and we restate ratio (4.2) as:

$$r = \frac{p[r][Y_\beta - Y_\alpha]}{p[r][K_\beta - (K_\alpha - K'_\alpha)]} \qquad 4.3$$

The assumption underlying the marginal productivity approach is that the calculated rate of profit resulting from changing the

quantity of capital will, for some levels of a predetermined
rate of profit be greater than it, while for some other
levels be less than it. The calculated rate of profit is
unique with regard to a particular technique of production,
where this technique is mirrored in the value of capital
per man in use.

On the surface it seems that in a realistic expression
such as ratio (4.3) we have nothing more than a mechanism for
making a choice between two techniques on the basis of some
existing rate of profit. But this mechanism serving as a
means to calculate a rate of profit, has somehow jumped the gap
to become a means to explain what determines the rate of
profit. The jump is easily (if erroneously) made by operating
ratio (4.3) as if it existed in our abstract one sector homogeneous goods world.

In the abstract case there is no complication of redundant
capital goods. Recalling our basic neoclassical construction,
this is taken care of by the malleability of capital assumption.
And in this one sector model, output is an all purpose output in that
while it serves as a consumption good, that portion of output
that is not consumed becomes part of the capital stock. Here
capital is not expressed in terms of a value of net output
by knowing the system of prices; in this homogeneous goods
case, net output and the capital good consists of the same
physical good (let us consider this good as corn output).

Assume a level of corn production with an α technique as
Y_{α}; and that a changeover to a β technique which will yield a
net output Y_{β} simply requires taking a certain physical quantity
of Y_{α} and adding it to the capital stock, and in doing do we
in no way alter the use of the amount of corn that was
previously saved and is the existing capital stock. The switch

91

from α to β means consuming less corn than previously in any once period in order to bring about a permanent increase in net output ($Y_\beta > Y_\alpha$). In this case we have ratio (4.4) which is nothing more than a restatement of ratio (4.3) in a setting where both denominator and numerator are composed of the same physical good, which frees the ratio from price considerations. Thus one calculates a rate of profit – a physical rate of profit – that results from this particular act of capital accumulation. We write:

$$R = \frac{Y_\beta - Y_\alpha}{Y_\alpha - \overline{Y}_\alpha} \qquad\qquad 4.4$$

($\overline{Y}_\alpha$ being the amount of corn saved out of Y_α).

But there does exist a rate of profit (r) reflective of Y_α; maintaining this level of output requires that a certain proportion of corn not be consumed. Should R < r then the technique which is the more profitable is the one which entails a lower capital per man, and if R > r it is the technique that is more capital intensive which is most profitable. Now suppose a third technique γ requiring additional accumulation and increasing the capital stock over that of β, and which yields a rate of profit R' such that R' < R. Proceeding with this line of reasoning, suppose a fourth technique δ with the same property of a higher level of capital per man when compared to γ as was β in a comparison with α, and calculate a rate of profit for δ as R" such that R" < R'. We have four techniques that can be ordered on the basis of an increased quantity of required capital or, which comes to the same ordering, on the basis of a decreasing physical rate of profit.

92

Comparing β and γ we see:

$$\frac{Y_\beta - Y_\alpha}{k_\beta - k_\alpha} > \frac{Y_\gamma - Y_\beta}{k_\gamma - k_\beta} \qquad\qquad 4.5$$

γ has more net product and capital than β, but
the ratio of product to capital for γ is less
than for β.

The differences between an existing rate of profit (r)
generated by a given technique, and the calculated rates of
profit resulting from other techniques requiring larger amounts
of capital, become increasingly greater. These differences
are non-reversible, for otherwise subsequent techniques will
see an increase in the rate of profit, with the possibility
that a technique characterized by some higher level of
capital per man will be as profitable as the earlier lower
capital intensive technique at some predetermined (r). And
on the other side, techniques which reduce the level of capital
per man will find calculated rates of profit exceeding that
of (r). We are saying that while a switchpoint may be
possible, there will only be a single rate of profit at
which such a point occurs as between any two techniques. There
is, in this abstract one commodity world, a very definite
negative ordering one either side of a switchpoint between the
physical rate of return and the quantity of capital per man.

We can express all this in figure (4.1).

Fig. 4.1

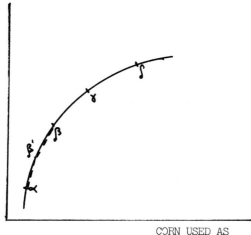

CORN OBTAINED AS
NET OUTPUT

CORN USED AS
CAPITAL GOOD

Let us suppose our four techniques, so that the economy is
represented by points α through δ. We see the rate of
profit declining as we ascend the hierarchy of techniques, and
this is reflected by the declining slope of the curve connecting
the four points. But two equi-profitable techniques are shown by
the dashed line segment such as αβ, indicating that the same
rate of profit can be obtained by either technique or by a combination of the two, i.e. being at a point of the segment.
Yet a technique β' can be developed between α and β, so that a
switchpoint αβ now becomes two switchpoints αβ' and β'β. For
example should the segment αβ be a switchpoint at 3%, we now
have further switchpoint in segment αβ' at 4%. And this can go

94

on by presuming a facet between α and β' at a rate greater
than 4%; until in the limit only one technique is the most
profitable at any one rate of profit. By assuming that
between any two techniques, no matter how small the amount
of capital difference, one can always interject a third, then
the techniques crowd together to form a smooth curve and
all flat segments become irrelevant. As Professor Pasinetti
points out "Any addition of corn to the means of production
(no matter how small) always makes the system change from
one technique to another, without ever,being at a switching
point."[2] Thus each technique becomes associated with a
particular rate of profit.

Of course, what we have here is the construction that
underpins marginal productivity of capital determination of the
rate of profit. But in saying this we commit the error
that continues to exert its influence; for what we should say
is the determination of the physical rate of profit, as this
analysis makes sense only in the one commodity abstract world.
We do find, in this context, that an increase in the accumulation
of capital (the act of saving corn) will increase net output per
unit of labor; but this change will be greater the lower the
existing stock of corn used as capital. That is, the less
mechanized the existing technique, the greater will be the
physical rate of return as a result of adding to the capital
stock (thus the inverse relation between the reward for
investment and the existing stock of capital). This physical
rate of return can be considered as the price of capital, thus
giving is an indicator of the quantity of capital.

What remains to be seen is how this whole construction
explaining the rate of profit in the infinite technique one
commodity world, has been promulgated to act as a surrogate

95

for an explanation of the rate of profit in a world where
output results from the input of labor and capital, and
where output and input are heterogeneous goods. We want to
redesign ratio (4.3) so as to have it fit the marginal
product explanation of ratio (4.4).

This is done by way of general acceptance of what
Professor Pasinetti refers to as an unobtrusive proposition.
This proposition has so widely been adopted as to become a
postulate, i.e. a proposition that is so evident as not to
need any discussion or justification. The postulate can be
stated as follows: if at a given rate of profit (r^*) two
techniques are equally profitable, then at a rate of profit
greater than this ($r>r^*$) the technique that becomes more
profitable is the one with a lower value of capital and
net output per unit of labor. To this postulate we need
only add the capital malleability assumption, which ensures
no wastage of capital in a change from one technique to another.
The capital stock is always appropriate to the most profitable
technique in use and is always fully employed. And one can,
as we have seen, make irrelevant points of technique switching
by tending the number of techniques to infinity, and having
all of them ordered according to the postulate. Thus we come
up with a smooth curve where changes in the rate of profit
imply inverse directional change in the value of capital.

Now these points convert ratio (4.3) to the following:

$$\P = \frac{p[r][Y_\beta - Y_\alpha]}{p[r][K_\beta - K_\alpha]} \qquad 4.6$$

which is similiar but not identicle to the abstract case.
Outputs and inputs are a collection of heterogeneous goods
and the calculated rate of profit ($\P$) depends on an existing

price system. Should a change in technique cause the calculated rate of profit to be less than the existing rate, it then tells us that the existing price structure corresponds to an existing profit rate (r) that is greater than a switch-point rate (r^*). The postulate does inform us that at $r > r^*$ the most profitable technique is one with a lower value of capital; so that a condition of $\P < r$ becomes associated with a technique that has a higher value of capital. And conversely, should $\P > r$ at an existing price system, it must mean that the given price system corresponds to an existing rate of profit such that $r < r^*$. Again, our assumption tells that condition $\P > r$ reflects a technique that has a lower value of capital. The point is, that as long as $\P \gtrless r$ at given prices, than the existing rate of profit cannot be a switchpoint rate. Since between any two techniques there can be only one switchpoint rate, we can then say that for $r > r^*$ the value of capital per man is lower than at $r = r^*$ and for condition $\P < r$ the value of capital exceeds that for (r). Also for $r < r^*$ the value of capital is greater than $r = r^*$, so that for $\P > r$ the capital value is lower than at (r). We have our inverse relation between the rate of profit and the value of capital per man on either side of a switchpoint. Thus the rate of profit cf ratio (4.6) which depends on a given price system and rate of profit, is made to behave like the rate of profit drawn from the abstract case of ratio (4.4). It is as if one were able to calculate the rate of profit independent of an existing rate of profit; to treat the value of capital as a quantity of an alike capital. We have in the resulting smooth inverse relationship, that only one "quantity of capital" (one kind of technique) becomes associated with one rate of profit. Let us listen

97

directly to Pasinetti on this point:

> "As the rate of profits consistently de-
> creased, the techniques which successively
> become the most profitable are associated
> with higher and higher values of capital
> per man (with higher and higher net
> outputs per man). The desired relation-
> ship is thereby made to emerge: 'quan-
> tity of capital' and rate of profit are
> inversely related to each other! The
> basic idea for which the infinite tech-
> nique one-commodity case has been con-
> structed is thereby extended to being
> a general feature of any economic
> system."[3]

So, in summary, what this extension does, is to allow
one to construct an aggregate production function for a
multi-type output economy in which quantities of capital
and labor produce a level of output, and by means of the
marginal product of the factors will also explain the
distribution of that output. A construction which
formed the core of our discussion in chapter 1, and which
was considered as the natural order of things. But we
were able to do this because the function was interpreted,
albeit unconsciously, as if it were that of our one output
abstract world.

Let us then reiterate the fundamental flaw; it is that
the accepted production function and the principles
extracted from it founder on the inability to consider capital
in the form of a magnitude that is independent of the
distribution of output. In subsequent chapters we continue
to chip away at the traditional theory before coming to a
"new" approach.

NOTES

1. We are guided by Professor Pasinetti's analysis in his "Switches of Technique and the 'Rate of Return' in Capital Theory", <u>Economic Journal</u>, September 1969. pp. 508–529.

2. Ibid., p. 518.

3. Ibid., p. 522.

5. SWITCHING AND RESWITCHING OF TECHNIQUES

We begin this chapter by working through a procedure to demonstrate the ordering of techniques according to least cost at different wage rates (which means that it is possible to have such an ordering at different rates of profit for the same wage rate); and that the switch to the cheaper (more profitable) technique will bring the economy to a higher wage rate (or to a higher rate of profit at the same wage rate).[1] Also, we will see that techniques giving the same wage rate are equally profitable at the given level of the rate of profit, and can be said to co-exist.

Making use of the two sector Hicksian system in chapter 3 we write:

$$K^\gamma = a^\gamma (rK^\gamma) + b^\gamma w^\gamma \qquad\qquad 5.1$$

$$C^\gamma = \alpha^\gamma (rk^\gamma) + \beta^\gamma w^\gamma \qquad\qquad 5.2$$

$$K^\delta = a^\delta (rk^\gamma) + b^\delta w^\gamma \qquad\qquad 5.3$$

$$C^\delta = \alpha^\delta (rk^\gamma) + \beta^\delta w^\gamma \qquad\qquad 5.4$$

The symbols a^γ, b^γ, α^γ and β^γ are the input coefficients per unit of output of the capital sector (K) and consumption sector (C) respectively, where the outputs are produced with a (γ) technique, i.e. K^γ, C^γ. Equations, (5.1, 5.2) show the value of the sectoral outputs based on the existing rate of profit and wage rate associated with the γ technique (w^γ). The term (K^γ) is the value of capital associated with (γ) technique prices.

Statements (5.3) and (5.4) give the value of the sector outputs where an alternative (δ) technique is in use, but with the inputs being costed at the prices associated with the original (γ) technique. Technique (δ) in terms of final product will be less or more costly than (γ) – at prices corresponding to γ – according as $C_\gamma^\delta \lessgtr C_\gamma^\gamma$ (C_γ^δ is the value of final good using (δ) technique but costed at (γ) technique prices, with C_γ^γ being the value of the good using (γ) technique and costed at (γ) prices).

Now let us turn matters around and assume that technique (δ) was originally in use with an associated (w^δ); and let (γ) be the alternative technique costed at the (δ) prices.

We have:

$$K^\delta = a^\delta \ (rK^\delta) + b^\delta w^\delta \qquad\qquad 5.5$$
$$C^\delta = \alpha^\delta \ (rK^\delta) + \beta^\delta w^\delta \qquad\qquad 5.6$$
$$K^\gamma = a^\gamma \ (rK^\delta) + b^\gamma w^\delta \qquad\qquad 5.7$$
$$C^\gamma = \alpha^\gamma \ (rK^\delta) + \beta^\gamma w^\delta \qquad\qquad 5.8$$

The consumption good can be produced with the γ or δ technique, and we come up with four values of the good due to the different techniques being costed at different prices. That is:

> γ technique at γ prices.
> γ technique at δ prices.
> δ technique at δ prices. $\qquad$ 5.9
> δ technique at γ prices.

For a given price system the different values stem from the different input coefficients, hence for a given technique, the sector values will reflect the difference in the price system – in our example we are talking about the difference in the wage rate at the same rate of profit. The ratio between prices and wages will be the same in both techniques, which we write as:

$$\frac{C^\delta_\gamma}{C^\delta_\delta} = \frac{w^\gamma}{w^\delta} = \frac{C^\gamma_\gamma}{C^\gamma_\delta} \qquad 5.10$$

From statement (5.10) we discern a uniform ordering of techniques as to least cost. For example, should technique (δ) be in use in the price situation corresponding to (δ), i.e. rw^δ, and it is determined that (δ) would be less costly at prices rw^γ, then we also see that should the (γ) technique have been in use, it would also have been more costly at w^δ than w^γ. When $C^\delta_\gamma < C^\delta_\delta$ then $C^\gamma_\gamma < C^\gamma_\delta$. And should the ($\delta$) technique be deemed less costly at an alternative (δ) then existing (γ) price system, we see that the (γ) technique would as well have been less costly at (δ) than (γ) prices; i. e. when $C^\delta_\delta < C^\delta_\gamma$, then $C^\gamma_\delta < C^\gamma_\gamma$. Thus at an existing ($\delta$) price both techniques are more costly than at a (γ) price system, and at an existing (γ) price system both techniques are less costly at the alternative (δ) price system. We see that the order of both techniques is the same at both price systems.

Having established the existence of less costly production at other than an existing price system, it can be shown via fig. (5.1) that a move to such chealer methods brings us to a technique giving the highest wage for the same rate of profit, or to the highest rate of profit for the same wage.

Fig. 5.1

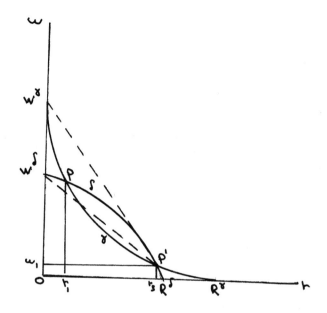

We see a double switching (reswitching) situation in which technique (γ) is more profitable than (δ) at profit rates below r_1 and above r_3; with technique (δ) being the more profitable at profit rates in-between. The switch to tne less costly technique entails a move to a higher wage which results in a wage curve given by $W^\gamma PP'R^\gamma$. At the switch or "corner" points we note $w_\gamma = w_\delta$ so that $c_\gamma^\gamma = c_\delta^\delta$; techniques giving the same wage are equally profitable. In moving off the switchpoint we come to a technique where $c_\delta^\delta < c_\gamma^\gamma$ for $w^\delta > w^\gamma$ (for profit rates between

103

r_1 and r_3).

At r_1 – with r rising – the switch is to technique (δ) which carries lower value of capital per head (in keeping with the traditional relationships); but at still higher levels of the rate of profit (beyond r_3) the switch is tc a technique with a higher degree of mechanization (and output per capita) – certainly not the expected association. This characteristic of the latter switch is evidenced by the slope of the lines drawn from P' to w^δ and w^γ.

To understand this geometric evidence we need to examine the particular wage curve for technique (γ) on a separate diagram.

Fig. 5.2

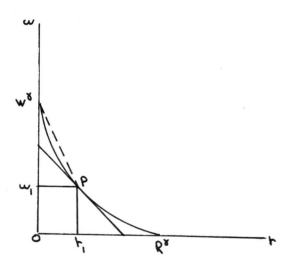

This wage curve tells us that the capital coefficient in the capital sector is less than that of the consumption sector, so that a rise in the rate of profit effects the cost of capital output less than it does consumption output. Pertaining to this technique one can write.

$$y = c + rk = c + gk \qquad 5.11$$

$$(g = \text{rate of growth})$$

dividing the output per head into net investment and consumption. At $r = 0$, the wage rate is at its maximum W^γ, and is reflective of a situation in which all net income goes to wages (corresponding to a maximum consumption output per head).

For a unit of consumption output there corresponds a level of capital production sufficient to replace the capital used up in the production of the consumption good, plus that which is necessary to replace the capital used to produce the capital imput to the consumption sector. Should net investment in the capital sector be zero, than total output consists of consumption output plus replacement of capital by the capital sector. In figure (5.2) the distance Ow^γ represents the output per unit of labor when such net investment is zero. Here we have the net product of the economy (output minus replacement of capital) consisting of consumption production only. Now the distance Ow_1 represents output per head where net investment in the capital sector is positive; output after replacement of capital exceeds production in the consumption sector – the economy increases its stock of machines. One can speak of the segment $W^\gamma w_1$ as showing that portion of consumption output sacrificed to permit net output of capital per head.

The tangent $w_1 PW^\gamma$ measures the value of capital per unit of labor at the wage Ow_1. We have:

105

$$w_1 P W^\gamma = \frac{w_1 W^\gamma}{w_1 P} = \frac{w_1 W^\gamma}{0 r_1} = \frac{profits}{rate\ of\ profits} \qquad 5.12$$

Note again that $0W^\gamma$ is net output when the rate of profit is zero, so that all net income goes to wages. The wage rate is the ratio of net income minus profits to the number of men employed; thus when $r = 0$, (w) is at maximum being equal to the value of net output per man. At the other extreme where $w=0$, the rate of profit is at maximum with all net income going to profits; the rate of profit being the ratio of net income minus wages to the value of the stock of capital. In this situation net output per man consists only of machines, and we have a rate of growth in the economy equal to that of the capital sector. For an intermediate position the value of net output consists of capital plus consumption goods, i.e. profits plus wages. That portion of it which consists of profits is $w_1 W^\gamma$, which then allows us to calculate the value of capital per man for that rate of profit (r_1) or for the counterpart wage rate (w_1). The greater the rate of profit, the greater the amount of net income going to profit (the flatter the tangent) and the greater the value of the stock per man.

In figure (5.1) we draw tangents to the two techniques at P' corresponding to $r_3 w_1$ to obtain the segments $P'w^\gamma$ and $P'w^\delta$ and find that:

$$w_1 P'W^\gamma > w_1 P'W^\delta$$

$$or \qquad 5.13$$

$$\frac{w_1 W^\gamma}{w_1 P'} > \frac{w_1 W^\delta}{w_1 P'}$$

106

At r_3 it is technique (γ) that is characterized by a higher
ratio of capital per man. Then at P' – with the rate of
profit rising – the switch to the most profitable technique
will bring us to the one with the higher wage rate which,
as we can see, is to technique (γ). But in doing so we have
also switched to the one with the higher capital and output
per head, as measured by $oW^\gamma > oW^\delta$. This move is in contrast
to the traditional relation between the rate of profit and the
value of capital per man.

At rates above r_3 it is technique (γ) that is in use, but
at rates below r_3 the switch is to (δ) which carries a lower
value of capital and output per man. This runs counter to the
accepted relationship; but equally upsetting is the fact, that
at still lower rates of profit, the economy will switch back
to a technique that had already been in use at some higher
rate of profit. It may be less than universally valid that,
should a particular technique be most profitable for a given
range of the rate of profit it will never reappear as the
best technique at another range.

II

Next we should like to understand why this reswitching
phenomenon may occur, now that we can appreciate the damage
that may result to traditional theory, and to the explanation
of relative income shares. Is reswitching an exceptional or
perverse happening?

We turn to the work of Bohm–Bawerk[2] to provide a framework
for the neoclassical result. Thereafter we will see what changes
in this framework can lead to the reswitching effect.

Assume a single productive factor (labor) producing a
single product, and that this input is applied in an "even-flow"
manner. The length of time between the first application of the

input and when the good is completed - ready for consumption -
is termed the period of production. The longer this period the
greater the increase of the final good output; though at some
point the further lengthening of this period will effect a
diminishing rate of increase to final output. This period
of production concept is a way to focus on the amount of
intermediate goods, i.e. capital goods, that (in an overall
sense) are used as inputs to support the production of the
end consumption output. The application of labor in the
production of an intermediate good can be viewed as the
application of labor a certain time period before the time
of the final output. Of course, an intermediate good can
itself be seen as a final good relative to the intermediate
goods that support it; but we carry on the discussion in
terms of a consumer good end product.

Now we turn to a calculation of Bohm-Bowerk's average
period of production. Say that we employ 4 units of labor in
each of three uniform periods of time, and then employ 2
units of labor for an additional fourth period of time (the
previous units of labor are not employed directly in the
activity of the fourth time period their labor is, so to speak,
passed on in the form of the capital good that is being worked
with in this period). And assume that it takes a total of five
periods for the final good to be produced. Each unit of labor
is to be multiplied by the difference between the total number
of production periods and the number of periods of its employment.
We can put this as the difference between the total production
time and that time period of the inputs "moment of application"
to the end product. For the four units of labor, their moment
comes at the end of three periods. The total number thus derived
is then divided by the total number of labor units to arrive at

the average period of production. Thus:

$$\frac{4 \cdot 2 + 2 \cdot 1}{6} = 1.7 \qquad\qquad 5.14$$

There are two extremes in this application of labor. One
is that all of the needed input is applied at the beginning of a
time period, and no further inputs are applied between this
period and when the final good becomes available. The second
is the even-flow process in which there is a uniformly spaced
application of labor; in each period of time from the initial
period to when the good is completed, there is an addition
of the same quantity of labor. In this even-flow case the
average period of production is equal to half the absolute
period of production, where this absolute period is the
total elapsed time between the period of the first application
of labor and that when the output is completed. As an
example, consider a production process composed of 7 time
periods with a uniform application of 7 units of labor. The
average period of production is: $\qquad\qquad$ 5.15

$$\frac{1 \cdot 6 + 1 \cdot 5 + 1 \cdot 4 + 1 \cdot 3 + 1 \cdot 2 + 1 \cdot 1 + 1 \cdot 0}{7} = 3$$

The last application of labor yields the final good, so that
from its point of view it is as if it produced the good. Of
course, it does so, but only in conjunction with the "ripened"
labor of each of the previous 6 stages as they are cumulatively
passed along to the last period of production.

The longer the average period of production i.e. the
greater the number of input periods, the greater the productivity
of labor at each period. We have a greater amount of capital
(intermediate goods) working with labor at each stage, and thus
passing on a greater production capability to the next stage.
And all this cumulating into a greater thrust of end product

output in the final period. The entire process is characterized
by a greater productivity of labor and a greater capital to
labor ratio. Now there exists at a point in time different
techniques of production with different amounts of capital
in their make-up (i.e. characterized by different average
periods of production, or, as it has been referred to, by
different degrees of roundaboutness); at an existing rate of
profit the economy seeks out the most profitable one.

Next we will need to understand Bohm-Bawerk's concept
of the subsistence fund and relate it to the average period of
production. One way to regard the fund is that it consists
of the stock of the intermediate outputs, the components of
which are at various stages removed from the final output.
From this view, one is sort of looking back from the end
product and seeing the fund as a stock of capital resulting
from the operation of a particular process (a technique
of a particular average period of production).

Yet another way is to view the fund as the source out of
which investment comes in order to put into operation a process
that yields a level of end product in the future. Here is one
looking forward and seeing the fund as a necessary source of
capital to sustain or start a productive process. The capital
stock as a result of investment provides output of end products
which is made available to labor, in order to sustain labor through
the intermediate stages of a subsequent process. The greater the
fund (the greater the stock of capital) the greater the stream of
final output which, then makes possible more elongated production
processes; since in this latter situation workers need to be
sustained with consumer goods for a longer time before such goods
become available.

Now we can get at the idea of an equilibrium rate of profit

110

and relate it to the wage rate.

Fig. 5.3

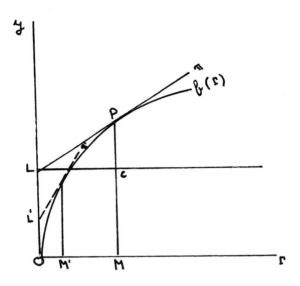

The economy invests a certain value of capital (representing
a given size of the subsistence fund) and thereby employs labor
with a technique of a particular average period of production.
In figure (5.3) we have a curve $f(\Gamma)$ which relates the productivity
of labor to (Γ) which is a measure of the elongation of the
production technique. There does exist a rate of profit, i.e. the
economy has realized a growth of the fund as a result of its
investment at a previous period, and we note this rate by the slope

111

of the line (L¶). A maximum rate of profit from investment
(from the employment of a particular roundabout process) is
achieved at point (P). At this point, the rate of profit
on the additional capital that makes possible the increase
in the average production period (and in output) is equal
to the average rate of profit. It is the point at which the
average rate of profit on capital is at maximum.

The wage rate is assumed given and equal to OL, so that
the total investment is OMCL (the investment, as we now have
come to consider it, is a sum that supports labor at a given
wage for a given employment level, i.e. for a certain average
period of production). The value of output stemming from this
investment is MP, with total wages being CM and total profits
equal to PC. The rate of profit is:

$$\frac{PC}{OL \cdot OM} \qquad\qquad 5.16$$

The investment of a fund size below OM will cause a rate of
profit in excess of a realized rate which, motivates the
investment of the now higher amount of profit bearing capital.
On an even-flow process the increase in the average period
of production means a proportional rise in investment, hence the
process is lengthened as investment absorbs the available
capital. An investment in excess of OM leads to a fall in the
rate of profit, and to the adoption of less elongated processes.
The maximum rate is reflected in the equality of the average and
marginal rates of return, as seen by the equality of the slopes of
both curves at (P). With the optimal technique determined the
economy then employs as many workers as the size of that fund
allows.

Suppose that the initial level of investment does not employ
all of the available labor; that is, at the existing wage rate

112

the fund size is insufficient to engage a period of production
large enough to result in full-employment. The investment that
is undertaken produces a relatively shorter period of production,
while at the same time the wage rate will fall. The economy
can be expected to self-adjust to full-employment as the lower
wage rate increases the ability of the fund to absorb a greater
level of employment. We have the adoption of labor intensive or
less roundabout production techniques; the lower wage rate motivates
the use of a smaller average period of production process that
indeed requires a fund smaller relative to the quantity of labor
employed. At full-employment we find a lower wage rate and a
shorter average period of production associated with a higher
rate of profit, as compared to a condition where the fund was
of a size sufficient to fully employ labor at the previous
higher wage rate. The optimum period of production is now OM'
with a higher rate of profit as given by the steeper curve
(L'¶'). For a fund of a given amount, there is a particular
wage rate that results in the existing rate of profit being an
equilibrium rate; such an equilibrium rate for a smaller fund
(relative to the employment of labor) is associated with a higher
rate of profit.

On the other hand, we can suppose a situation where at a
given wage rate the existing fund size is not fully used. That
is, the current technique is of a too short an average period
of production; increasing investment will be forthcoming which
will elongate the production technique and compete for employment
to carry out the greater number of production periods. Here
it is not a matter of excess labor but one of excess investment
capital relative to the existing labor force at the given wage
rate. We now find techniques brought into use that are of a
higher production period concommittant with a higher wage rate.
Indeed, the techniques that are motivated to be brought into play

113

are those requiring the very existence of the greater subsistence fund. In this equilibrium condition we find a higher average period of production, a greater quantity of capital and a higher wage rate; but we have a lower equilibrium rate of profit as compared to a condition of a smaller fund fully employing the labor force at a lower wage rate.

One can set out the inverse relation between the wage rate and the degree of roundaboutness of production. As we pointed out, should a technique reflect unemployment and a fall in the wage rate (a rise in the rate of profit), the system will move in the direction of less roundabout procedures; and this requires a fund (capital stock) that is small relative to the employed labor force. Thus a low wage rate ("high" rate of profit) relates to the existence of a low capital to labor ratio. Now the crux of the matter is that if at a certain rate of profit a particular average period of production exists, a change in the rate will induce a different roundabout procedure; and the original procedure can never reappear unless the original rate of profit reappears. A fund size that relates to one wage rate (to one degree of roundaboutness) cannot come back to be the capital stock relating to another wage rate. We have the impossibility of reswitching and thereupon the entire neoclassical edifice.

This whole notion of the size of the fund as an index of the average period of production, allows us to think of this capital stock as given independent of distribution. We have something that we can take the marginal product of as a result of a change in the elongation of production. But it is this thought process that has caused much difficulty. The point is, that given the rate of profit one can calculate the

114

size of the fund and the average period of production; but
then one cannot use the average period of production to
determine the rate of profit and the distribution of income.

We should not perceive the capital structure as appearing,
so to speak, out of the blue, and employing itself with a
particular technique. And, at a later time, it appears again
of a different size and is employed with a different technique
reflecting a different average period of production. This fund
that serves to employ labor is shown to be of different lengths of
production in response to varying wage rates; but it is not
handled as an input in the make-up of its own size. Yet the
degree of roundaboutness in one period effects the relation
of capital to labor in another period. The average period
of production (as it reflects the value of capital) cannot be
treated as datum external to the productive system itself.

Consider a situation where output results from the inputs
of land and labor, but no capital is required. Let a_X and a_L
be the inputs of land and labor needed to produce a unit of
output (Y) using technique (A); and that b_X and b_L be the
respective inputs using technique (B). Also that p_X and p_L
be the rates of rent and wages. The ratio of the cost of using
$A(p_A)$ to that of using techniqe B (p_B) is:

$$\frac{p_A}{p_B} = \frac{a_X p_X + a_L p_L}{b_X p_X + b_L p_L} \qquad 5.17$$

which can be restated as:

$$\frac{p_A}{p_B} = \frac{\dfrac{a_X}{a_L} \cdot \dfrac{p_X}{p_L} + 1}{\dfrac{b_X}{b_L} \cdot \dfrac{p_X}{p_L} + 1} \cdot \frac{a_L}{b_L} \qquad 5.18$$

115

We see that a knowledge of the techniques is sufficient to
give the inputs, we are considering quantities of alike
physical inputs; and also that the cheaper or costlier technique follows upon the relative prices of the inputs. For
example, should $\frac{a_X}{a_L} > \frac{b_X}{b_L}$ and p_X fall by more than p_L, then

$\frac{p_A}{p_B}$ falls. Thus at relative higher labor costs (lower land rate)

the cheaper technique is one that uses a greater quantity of land
relative to labor (now if only we can say with equal certainty
that at a lower rate of profit the cheaper technique is one
that entails a higher value of capital, but, as we have seen,
this cannot always be said). Applying numbers to statement (5.18)
will make clear the relation that a fall in rent relative to
the wage results in relatively cheapening the land intensive
technique. Beginning with $\frac{a_X}{a_L} = \frac{8}{2}$, $\frac{b_X}{b_L} = \frac{6}{3}$ and $\frac{p_X}{p_L} = \frac{3}{2}$, then

$\frac{p_A}{p_B} = 1.17$ but should the input cost ratio fall to $\frac{p_X}{p_L} = \frac{2}{1.5}$, then

$\frac{p_A}{p_B} = 1.15.$ Or if we go the other way, and assume that the wage rate

goes up by less than rent we would find that the cheaper technique is
the labor intensive one. Should the factor price ratio be $\frac{p_X}{p_L} = \frac{5}{3}$

(rising to 1.7), then the cost ratio is $\frac{p_A}{p_B} = 1.17.$

Relating this outcome to our discussion of the choice of
roundaboutness, it is as if we were saying that labor is the only
input. An increase in the wage rate will see the adoption of more
roundabout procedures; choosing the less costly technique means the
one that is more capital intensive. A decrease in the wage (increase

in the rate of profit) is associated with the technique
of a lower value of capital. We apply the results of a
situation in which both capital and labor are inputs. But this
does not work out; once capital is treated as a flexible input
our ordered inverse relation can go awry - reswitching is a
possibility. The Bohm-Bowerk framework has to be abandoned
as a result of our understanding that the average period of
production cannot be taken independent of the distribution of
income.

What happens if we replace the land input with that of
value of capital? Well, as we discussed previously, we cannot
determine what constitutes a value of capital as an approximation of a physical input "capital" without first knowing the
productive technique and the distribution of income under which
this input is produced. This input is now a product of the
system, and like any other product, its value will change with
changes in the relation between the rate of profit and the
wage rate. A calculation of the value of capital (as given
by (Γ) will then require the use of a compound profit formula.

However, let us first solve for a (Γ) under the Bohm-
Bowerk assumption of simple profit. Suppose we supply a unit of
labor in each stage of a two stage process, and a rate of
profit is earned over the two stages (but where the value of the
input is not effected by an existing rate of profit). We have:

$$L(1+2r) + L(1+r) = 2L(1+\Gamma r)$$
$$2L+3Lr = 2L+\Gamma r \qquad\qquad 5.19$$
$$r = 1.5$$

But the solution for (Γ) must account for the fact that the
value of capital input for which a rate of profit is earned
is itself indeterminate unless calculated at a rate of profit.
We need to express matters as:

$$L(1+r)^2 + L(1+r) = 2L(1+r)^\Gamma \qquad\qquad 5.20$$

dividing by L and multiplying gives:
$$r^2 + 3r + 2 = 2 (1+r)^\Gamma \qquad\qquad 5.21$$

and solving by logs:
$$\log(r^2+3r+2) = \log 2 + \Gamma\log(1+r)$$

$$\Gamma = \frac{\log(r^2+3r+2) - \log 2}{\log (1+r)} \qquad\qquad 5.22$$

The expression for (Γ) contains the rate of profit, and we are
back to the circularity of reasoning encountered in previous
discussions. To reiterate, it is the rate of profit that is to
be determined, and it is presumably a function of the roundaboutness of production; but we now find that the value of the capital
input as reflected in this roundaboutness, is seen to be dependent
on the rate of profit.

This uncoupling of the expected inverse ordering between
rate of profit and capital intensity throws serious doubt, as
we indicated, upon the neoclassical explanation for distribution,
and we will want to come up with another approach to the matter.
But at this point we go on to a further adjustment of neoclassical
premises by seeing what happens when labor is applied non-uniformly
over production processes.

III

Suppose process (A) that is of two periods using 7 units of
labor in the first period and none in the second; and a three period
process (B) employing 2 units of labor in the first period, none
in the second and 6 units of labor in the third (which is less than
the total labor input of the entire (A) process). We have two
techniques that employ labor non-uniformly, are of different lengths
of production and produce the same quantity of output. It can be
shown that the ratio of the cost of production $\frac{p_B}{p_A}$ will be above

and then fall below unity depending on the values for the rate of

118

profit.[3]

At high values for (r) - negligible wage costs - the
profit of employing the 2 units of labor in the first period,
when added to the labor in the third period calculated again
at the (r) rate, will yield a total cost that exceeds the
wage and profit of the less labor using technique. Also at
low levels of the rate of profit the (A) technique is again
least cost because it uses the lowest total input of labor
over all of the production periods. But there is an intermediate
range of the rate of profit where the profit on profit of the
investment of B's labor makes the total cost of this process
less than that of (A) even though (B) uses more labor in
total.

Now to an example of this. Suppose we produce a unit of
champagne with the (A) technique requiring an investment of
7 units of labor in the first period to produce a unit of
brandy, and that in one more period the brandy ferments by
itself into a unit of champagne. The cost of the champagne
is the cost of the brandy reckoned at the given (r) plus the
profit on the cost, i.e. it is the profit on profit of the
investment of the 7 units of labor. Thus:

$$1(1+r) + r(1+1r) \qquad\qquad 5.23$$
at r=100% (r=1) and wage rate = 1 then:
$$7(1+1) = 1(7+7) = 28$$

The value of the champagne consists of an intermediate capital
cost of 14 plus a 100% profit on that cost.

As an alternative we can produce this champagne with the
(B) technique that requires and investment of 2 units of labor
in the first period to produce one unit of grapejuice which
in one further period will ferment by itself into a unit of wine.
In a third period there is an investment of 6 units of labor to

119

turn this wine into champagne. The cost via this procedure
is, first of all, that of the investment of the 2 units of
labor plus a rate of profit on this investment, we have $2
wages plus $2 profits $[2 \cdot 1 + r(2 \cdot 1)]$; secondly the cost of the
wine, which is the cost of the juice plus the rate of
profit on this cost $[4(1+1)]$; and lastly the investment of
this $8 plus a direct input of $6 worth of labor, all
reckoned at the 100% rate of profit which gives a final cost
of $[6+8 \ (1+1)] = \$28$.

   Both techniques are of equal cost $\frac{p_B}{p_A} = 1$. Now we try
a lower rate of profit of 10% while assuming no change in the
wage of labor. The cost of using the (A) technique is
$7(1+.10) = 7.7$, while that of (B) is 9.26. The latter being
composed of the cost of the juice of $2(1+.10) = 2.2$, that
of the wine equal to $2.2 \ (1+.10) = 2.42$ leading to the cost
of the final output of $[(6+2.42) \ (1+.10)] = 9.26$. In fact
we find that for a range of the rate of profit from very low
to 50% the cost ratio is $\frac{p_B}{p_A} > 1$ (at zero rate of profit

technique (A) has to be less costly since it uses less labor
overall). At 50% the cost ratio is unity at 15.75, and for
a range in excess of 50% to 100% the ratio falls below unity.
For example, at $r = 70\%$ we find $p_A = 20.23$ and $p_B = 20.02$.
And for rates in excess of 100% we have, once again, that
$\frac{p_B}{p_A} > 1$.

   The effect of rate of profit changes on relative costs as
summarized in figure (5.4).

Fig. 5.4

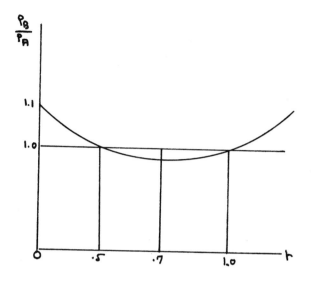

Relating this view of reswitching to the time length of production, we find that the technique which is least costly and adopted at low rates of profit, and which comes back to be used at high rates of profit, uses less time and less labor overall. Thus it is not, as would be supposed from the Bohm-Bowerk framework, that as the rate of profit falls the technique brought into use would always be one with the longer time length, requiring the existence of a capital stock larger relative to the quantity of labor. We now have the non-uniform application of labor as

121

another factor that makes suspect the traditional relationship between rate of profit and capital intensity.

This reswitching example is that of a circulating capital type, in which the capital as it circulates through time to be operated upon by different quantities of labor, changes its form on the way to becoming the final good. Now we want to observe reswitching in a durable (fixed) capital model, where it results from different present value calculations. Suppose we have two machines (A) and (B) that yield different quantities of output over different time spans, and let output sell for $1.00 per unit. Machine (A) yields an output value of 18 one period after it is put in place and a value of 54 at the end of three periods. While machine (B) gives an output value of 63 at the end of two periods.

For the present discount value of these income streams to be equal and choice between them indifferent, we need a rate of profit such that:

$$\frac{18}{1+r} + \frac{54}{(1+r)^3} = \frac{63}{(1+r)^2} \qquad 5.24$$

Equation (5.24) will hold four r's of 50% and 100%. For rates of profit below 50% machine (A) yields the higher present discounted value and is preferred. For example, at the extreme of $r = 0\%$ the value of (A) is 72 exceeding that of (B); and for $r = 25\%$ the discounted value of A's output stream is 46.09 while that for (B) is 40.38. At $r = 50\%$ we have A = B = 28.

for r's between 50% and 100% it is (B) that is preferred. at $r = 100\%$ both are again equal at a discounted value of 15.75, but at $r > 100\%$ machine (A) comes back with the higher value and is preferred to (B).

Both capital models give the reswitching phenomenon under assumptions which certainly cannot be considered outlandish.

Returning to the circulating capital example, we can say
that at r = .5 both techniques are able to pay a wage rate
of one dollar. In our example, the cost ratio changes as a
result of a change in the rate of profit; yet for a given
technique along its corresponding wage curve, a change in the
rate of profit will alter the wage rate. Though a preferred
technique is usually started as one which, for the given wage,
yields the highest rate of profit; it can also be viewed as one
which, for the given rate of profit, yields the highest wage
rate. We turn to an example that shows reswitching in terms
of the wage rate and the rate of profit.[4]

Fig. 5.5

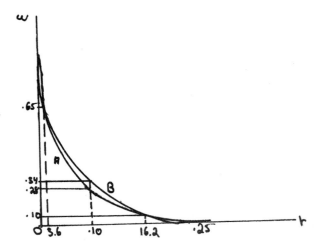

There are two technologies capable of producing a final good.
Technology (A) has a production length of 9 periods, and requires an

123

input of .8 of the final good in period 0 when the end product emerges; and also an investment of 20 units of labor in the first period of the process, i.e. 8 periods before period 0, or in period (-8). The (B) technology requires .8 of the final good plus 24 units of labor in period 0, and an input of 1 unit of labor in period (-25) [this technology having a gestation of 26 periods].

Considering the (A) approach, we find the value of the intermediate output at the end of (-8) as:

$$20w_A \ (1+r) \qquad\qquad 5.25$$

w_A = wage rate with A technique

and at the end of 7 periods before that of final output (-7) as:

$$[20w_A \ (1+r)] \ (1+r) \qquad\qquad 5.26$$

or

$$20(1+r)^2 w_A$$

and so on to the value in the period before period 0 as:

$$20(1+r)^8 w_A \qquad\qquad 5.27$$

with the value of the final good (p_A^0) being:[5]

$$p_A^0 = \frac{20(1+r)^8}{1-.8 \ (1+r)} \cdot w_A \qquad\qquad 5.28$$

For technology (B) the value of the final good is:

$$p_B^0 = 1w_B \ (1+r)^{25} + 24w_B + .8p_B \ (1+r)$$

$$= \frac{1(1+r)^{25}+24}{1-.8(1+r)} \cdot w_B \qquad\qquad 5.29$$

We can express the wage rate in each technology in terms of the final good. Setting the price of the final good equal to unity, $p_A^0 = p_B^0 = 1$, we can then directly compare the two techniques with regard to which gives the higher wage rate –

in terms of command over the final good - for any given rate
of profit. We have a relation between the rate of profit and
the wage rate for each technique as:

$$w_A = \frac{1-.8(1+r)}{2_0(1+r)^8} \qquad 5.30$$

$$w_B = \frac{1-.8(1+r)}{(1+r)^{25}+24} \qquad 5.31$$

There are three rates of profit at which both systems
are equally profitable. At $r = 3.6\%$ both yield a wage rate of
.65, at $r = 16.2\%$ we find $w_A = w_B = .10$ and at $r = 25\%$ $w_A = w_B = 0$.
At a rate of profit of 10% it is technique (B) that is most
profitable, in that it gives a higher wage rate in terms of
profuct then (A); we find $w_A = .28$, $w_B = 34$. Of course,
another way to reckon this, is that at a wage rate common to
both techniques say at .34, (B) is preferable in that it
pays this wage rate and yields a higher rate of profit than (A).
We note that at rates of profit in excess of 16.2%, technique
(A) is chosen; it does yield the higher wage rate for any given
rate of profit (it is also the preferred technique at rates of
profit less than 3.6%).

Still another way to guage technique preference is to observe
that for a wage rate - rate of profit relationship - where (r)
runs from 0 to 3.6%, production with the (A) technique yields the
higher price for the final good. From 3.6% to 16.2% we find
$p_A^o - p_B^o < 0$, and from 16.2% to 25% technique (A) comes back, as
$p_A^o - p_B^o > 0$.

If we take the extreme of $r = 0$, then all of the value of
output goes to labor. From equations (5.30) and (5.31) we read

the wage rates as $w_A = 1.0$, $w_B = 0.8$; final output per unit of labor given by (A) is higher than (B). In a condition where the wage rates are the same, profits per man would then be higher for technology (A). But such a switchpoint condition also means identicle rates of profit, for which it follows that the value of capital per man for (A) must be higher than for (B).

This tells us that for rates of profit in excess of 3.6% (the first switchpoint) to a rate of 16.3%, the switch has been to a technology with a lower total value of capital per man, and that at a profit rate in excess of 16.2% (the second switchpoint) the switch is back to a technology with a higher value of capital per man - back to the technique that was preferred at profit rates below 3.6%.

This discussion, perhaps more vividly, reinforces our overall conclusion that, "at any given state of technical knowledge, switches of techniques due to changes in the rate of profit do not allow us to make any general statement on changes in the 'quantity of capital' per unit of labor. The new technology may require a lower 'quantity of capital' per unit of labor, whether capital is measured in terms of values or in terms of any chosen physical unit, whether we consider any single industry or the economic system as a whole."[6] The rate of profit can therefore no longer give an assured signal about the abundance or scarcity of capital with the most profitable technique.

Our reswitching examples would lead us to conclude that we are not dealing with unusual or exceptional happenings; but what is perhaps exceptional are the underlying premises of traditional theory. Other facets of this reswitching phenomenon are considered in the next chapter, as we move to further clear the air so that we can pose the question: just what does determine the rate of profit on the existing stock of capital?

126

NOTES

1. The basis for this is Professor Garegnani's note #1 in his article "Heterogeneous Capital, the Production Function and the Theory of Distribution" Review of Economic Studies, vol. 37, 1970, pp. 407-36. Equations (5.17) and (5.18) later in this chapter are drawn from his "Switching of Techniques", Quarterly Journal of Economics, vol. LXXX, pp. 554-67.

2. We are referring to the "Austrian school's" theory of capital. An illuminating discussion of the Bohm-Bawerk system in Friedrich A. Lutz, The Theory of Interest, Aldine, Chicago, 1968. Chapter I.

3. We follow Samuelson's illustration, in his "A Summing Up", Quarterly Journal of Economics, 1966, pp. 568-83. vol. LXXX.

4. This example is drawn from L. L. Pasinetti, "Changes in the Rate of Profit and Switches of Techniques", Quarterly Journal of Economics, vo. LXXX, pp. 503-17.

5. The value of the final output contains .8 value of final output already produced, thus:

$$p_A^O = 20(1+r)^8 w_A + .8 \ p_A^O \ (1+r)$$

$$p_A^O = [1-.8(1+r)] = 20 \ (1+r)^8 w_A$$

$$p_A^O = \frac{20(1+r)^8}{1-.8(1+r)} \cdot w_A$$

6. Pasinetti, op. cit., p. 514

6. WICKSELL EFFECTS AND DISTRBUTION

Consider a reswitching setting in fig. (6.1) where we have two techniques (A,B) differing their wage rate - rate of profit configuration.

Fig. 6.1

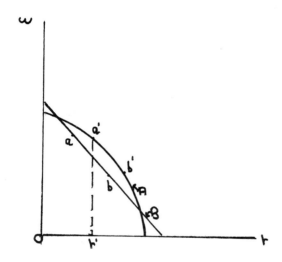

Corresponding to a rate of profit (r') it is technique (A) that is in use, and we have a particular cost of capital reflective of this distribution of income and technique. The effect of a change in the w-r relationship that is not associated with the adoption of a different technique (a move from a' to b') is

called the Price Wicksell Effect. We are talking about a
change in the value of capital as it relates to a change in (w)
and (r) for the given time-pattern of production, or, in
Joan Robinson's way, for the given real capital in terms of
labor time. Now this effect may be positive, negative or
neutral, depending on the sign for (m) that characterizes
the technique.

When $m = 1$ (the linear wage curve of technique B) the
factor ratios are the same in both the consumption and
capital good sectors. A change in the rate of profit will
leave relative costs of production unchanged, and the
sectoral price ratio uneffected. Recall that we have two
elements in costs, the wage rate and the rate of profit,
which vary in opposite directions on a factor-price curve.
A move from point a to b on the (B) technique curve is one
of the nuetral Price Wicksell Effect. We illustrate this by
the following example.[1]

Suppose technique (B) produces output of 3 tons (t) of
wheat and 4 tons of copper in a manner that results in a
net output of 1 ton of wheat, using in total, 1 unit of labor
input. The input - output relationships are:

1t. wheat + 2.8 copper + .6 labor = 3t. wheat   6.1

1t. wheat + 1.2 copper + .4 labor = 4t. copper 6.2

We note that should the rate of profit be zero, then
all of the net output goes to wages. Since we use 1 unit of
labor, the wage rate gets translated into 1 unit of wheat, so
that total wages in terms of wheat equals the net output of
wheat. Let us rewrite equation (6.1) with the price of labor
in terms of wheat:

1t. wheat + 2.8 copper + .6 wheat = 3t. wheat   6.3
Next we need only to find the price of copper in terms of
wheat, thus putting all inputs and outputs on the same
base. Using equation (6.2) we obtain:

$$4 \text{ copper} - 1.2 \text{ copper} = 1.4 \text{ wheat} \qquad 6.4$$

$$\text{copper} = \frac{1.4}{2.8} = .5$$

The price ratio is 1t. copper = 5t. wheat.
We can now get at the capital to labor ratio in each
sector; but as capital is measured in terms of wheat, what we
are seeing is a ratio of wheat to labor. For the wheat
sector:

$$1t. \text{ wheat} + 1.40t. \text{ wheat} + .6L = 3t. \text{ wheat} \qquad 6.5$$

$$\text{and } \frac{K}{L} = \frac{2.40}{.6} = 4$$

For the copper (capital) sector:

$$1t. \text{ wheat} + .60 \text{ wheat} + .4L = 2t. \text{ wheat} \qquad 6.6$$

$$\text{and } \frac{K}{L} = \frac{1.60}{.4} = 4$$

The wage equation can be obtained from the value
equation for capital, we have:

$$(1.60)(1+r) + .4w = 2 \qquad 6.7$$

$$w = \frac{.40 - 1.6r}{.4} = 1 - 4r$$

with the wage curve anchored at the extremes of $r = 0$, $w = 1$
and $w = 0$, $r = .25$. At this maximum rate of profit, the value
of capital in terms of wheat is 4t. wheat; it is also this
value at the point $r = 0$, in fact, in this linear case the
value of capital is invariant to all values of the rate of
profit between zero and .25. At an arbitrary rate of $r = .10$,
the wage rate is .60, with the capital to labor cost ratio for

the wheat and copper sector being:

$$(\text{wheat}) \; \frac{2.64}{.36} = (\text{copper}) \; \frac{1.76}{.24} = 7.3 \qquad 6.8$$

with the value ratio of the wheat to copper sector as $\frac{3}{2}$. At a higher rate r = 20, the wage rate is .20, and the sector input cost ratios are:

$$(\text{wheat}) \; \frac{2.88}{.12} = (\text{copper}) \; \frac{1.92}{.08} = 24 \qquad 6.9$$

with sector cost ratio unchaged at $\frac{3}{2}$. This shows that if both sectors have the same capital to labor coefficients, then the rise in one element of cost just offsets the fall in the other, and relative prices are unaffected. So, to reiterate, the essential point is that as the rate of profit changes the value of capital remains the same.

A similar move from a' to b' along curve (A) which has a capital to labor ratio that is greater in the capital sector relative to the consumption sector (m<1), will find that increases in the rate of profit results in increases in the value of capital.[2] The higher rate of profit increases costs more in the technique which uses a higher proportion of capital to labor, and thereby results in a higher value of capital in terms of net product. This association between the value of capital and rate of profit for a given technique is referred to as a negative Price Wicksell Effect. On the other hand, a move along a technique curve characterized by the ratio of capital to labor being higher in the consumption sector (m>1), will find the value of capital falling as the rate of profit takes on higher values. This inverse relation is termed a positive Price Wicksell Effect.

But let us view these effects another way.[3] The value
accounting identity for the net product per unit of labor
flowing from a given technique is:

$$y = w + rk$$
$$\text{and} \qquad\qquad 6.10$$

$$w = \frac{y - rk}{L}, \; k = \frac{y - w}{r}$$

At the maximum wage rate, all net output goes to wages, i.e.
$w = w_{max} = W = y$. At the other intercept, the value of net
output goes to profits. When $r = r_{max} = R$ we find:

$$r = \frac{y}{k} \qquad\qquad 6.11$$

the rate of profit is equal to the ratio of net output to
the stock of capital.

Corresponding to these value statements, there are intercepts of a curve mirroring the physical side of output. Thus:

$$y = c + gk$$
$$(g - \text{growth of capital}) \qquad\qquad 6.12$$
$$\text{and}$$

$$k = \frac{y - c}{g}$$

When $r = 0$, the value of output per man coincides with the
maximum consumption per man; so that when $w = y$, we have $y = c = C$
and $gk = 0$. And when $r = R$ the ratio $\frac{y}{k}$ coincides with (g),
giving the maximum growth of capital (G), i.e. $Gk = y$. Another
way to state these relationships is to write (6.12) as:

$$k = \frac{c}{\frac{y}{k} - g} \qquad\qquad 6.13$$

(the denominator being the ratio of output of consumption
good to that of capital).

132

The value of capital per man at the extreme rates of
profit, for a given growth rate g, can be stated (from 6.12
and 6.13) as:

$$k_{r=o} = \frac{C-c}{g}, \quad k_{r=R} = \frac{c}{G-g} \qquad 6.14$$

Fig. 6.2

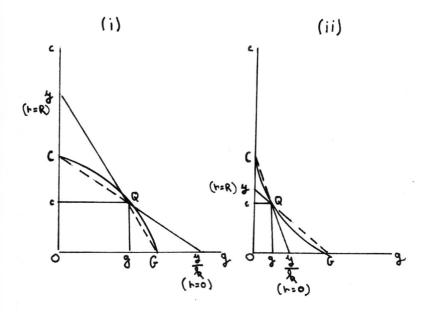

We have a consumption curve CG on which we choose a point Q
corresponding to g and c. First we consider the value of
capital per man at the point r = 0. Here (y) coincides with
(C), and the value of capital is measured by the slope of the
line from C to Q, i.e. by the ratio $\frac{C-c}{g}$. Note than an extension
of the line CQ to the horizontal axis gives the value of output/

133

capital ratio when $r = 0$. Now checking these values for
the convex consumption curve $(m>1)$, we find a value for (k)
that is at maximum and a value for $(\frac{y}{k})$ that is at minimum
as compared to a minimum (k) and maximum $(\frac{y}{k})$ in the condition
of the concave consumption curve when the rate of profit is
zero. Thus increase in the rate of profit will find (k)
increasing and $(\frac{y}{k})$ decreasing when the consumption curve is
concave, and (k) decreasing and the ratio of output to
capital increasing when the consumption curve is convex.

Looking at matters at the other extreme of $r = R$, we
find the value of capital per man given by the slope of the
line from G to Q, i. e. by the ratio $\frac{c}{G-g}$. Here $\frac{y}{k}$ coincides
with G, and by extension of GQ to the verticle axis we get
the value of net output per man when the rate of profit is
at maximum. The value of capital per man is at maximum
at the extreme of the maximum rate of profit in the
condition of the concave consumption curve, and is at
minimum in the condition of the convex curve. Thus when
the rate of profit falls, the value of (k) and that of (y)
will fall when it is the capital goods sector that is more
capital intensive; and the values of (k) and (y) increase
when it is the consumption sector that has the higher capital
to labor ratio.

It will be helpful to perform the same operation from
the point of view of taking an arbitrary rate of profit (r),
and seeing the values for k, y and $\frac{y}{k}$ at the extremes of the
growth rate (using a wage curve). The counterpart equations
to (6.14) are:

$$k_{g=0} = \frac{W-w}{r}, \ k_{g=G} = \frac{w}{R-r} \ . \qquad 6.15$$

Fig. 6.3

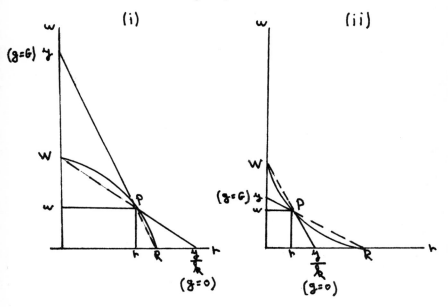

When g = 0, we have (y) coinciding with (W), and be extension
of the line WP to the horizontal axis we get at the value of
output to capital when net investment is zero. The value of
(k) is at mimimum and that of $(\frac{y}{k})$ at maximum under the
condition of m<1, as compared to a maximum of (k) and a
minimum of $(\frac{y}{k})$ when m>1. Hence a positive growth rate
will see higher values of (k) and lower values for $(\frac{y}{k})$
when m<1, and the reverse when m>1.

At the extreme of maximum growth of capital (G), the

value of capital per man is given by the slope of the line (PR), with the extension to the verticle axis showing (y). We note that in this condition the value of capital per man is at maximum and that of net output per man also at maximum when m<1, while both values are at minimum when m>1. Hence a fall in the growth rate will see a higher value of (k) when m>1 and a lower value of (k) when m<1.

Let us reiterate the basic idea that in moving along a wage curve for a given growth rate, we are getting at the difference in the value of the capital good associated with the difference in the rate of profit.

Now we turn to the idea of Real Wicksell Effects. Here we relate a change in the value of capital per man to a change in the technique of production, where this latter change is associated with a change in the rate of profit. A change in technique implies a change in the "quantity" of capital per man (in terms of end product); we have, in other words, a comparison of different average periods of production. This real effect is a composit of two influences; that of the change in the rate of profit and hence in the market value of the method of production, and that which reflects changes in the method itself. We are considering changes in (k) on either side of a switch-point.

A positive real effect is one where the more mechanized technique comes into play at a lower than switchpoint rate of profit. Here, in what is alo referred to as a forward switch, we find that the lower rate of profit cheapens the more capital intensive technique. We view this effect in fig. (6.4) at $(\bar{r})$.

Fig. 6.4

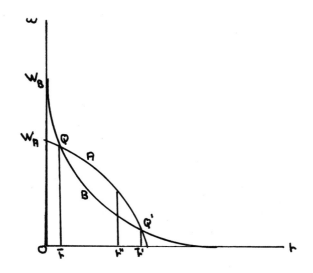

Technique (B) is the more producitve technique; it operates
with a higher value of capital and output per man. This is
seen by comparing the slope of a tangent drawn to technique
(B) at Q with that of technique (A). Now both techniques pay
the same wage rate and rate of profit at the switchpoint Q,
hence (A) must be earning a smaller amount of profit. And
for this smaller profit to translate into the same rate of
profit, the value of capital for (A) must be correspondingly
smaller (as it is reflective of a lower order of mechanization
in the production of the consumer good). The lower rate of

137

profit reduces costs by more in technique (B); it is the more profitable in that it can allow a higher wage rate than (A) for a rate of profit below $(\bar{r})$. We can see that labor equipped with the (B) technology is more productive than (A), since in the extreme $W_B > W_A$. At point Q' we have a negative real effect or backward switch. For a rate of profit lower than the switchpoint $(\bar{r}')$, the switch is to a technique with a lower value of capital and output per man.

The operation of a technique requiring a greater quantity of capital implies a greater growth rate of capital, and thereby the production of more machines. Going back to fig. (6.3) we see what a change in the growth rate entails directly for (k); it does call for a different stock of capital goods to produce the different combination of capital and consumption goods. This change in the value of capital stemming from a change in the growth rate - at a given rate of profit - is considered as the composition effect. The real Wicksell Effect relates the overall outcome of both consumption and price effects.

In fig. (6.3i) we see that a decline in the growth rate entails a decline in the value of (k); hence at a rate of profit below $(\bar{r}')$ in fig. (6.4) the switch is to a technique requiring a smaller growth rate of capital, we then get the negative composition effect that is reinforced by a negative price effect. At point Q, the switch is to a technique requiring the existence of a higher growth rate of capital giving a positive composition effect that is here reinforced by a positive price effect.

II

The associated equilibrium values of the two technique at a switchpoint are:

138

$$y_B = w + rk_B \qquad\qquad 6.16$$

$$y_A = w + rk_A$$

By subtraction we get:

$$\frac{y_B - y_A}{k_B - k_A} = r \qquad\qquad 6.17$$

the left side of (6.17) is the ratio of the change of the
stream of net output to that of of the value of capital (both
capital and output priced in terms of the same consumption
good) in a comparison of two techniques at one and the same rate
of profit. The techniques are equi-profitable in that the
amount left over after paying profits at the given rate,
allows the payment of the same wage rate. Another way of
saving the same thing is that at a given wage rate both
techniques have the same ratio of net output to the value of
capital.

Of course, technique (B) incorporates a greater amount of
capital and is more productive; we see $W_B > W_A$ (in terms of output
$y_B > y_A$), and can express this as:

$$\frac{y_B - w}{k_B} = \frac{y_A - w}{k_A} = r \qquad\qquad 6.18$$

so that:

$$y_B - y_A = r(k_B - k_A) \qquad\qquad 6.19$$

What we have in (6.17) is a ratio of profitability[4] between two

139

techniques, as this ratio is compared to an arbitrarily
given rate of profit. When this ratio is equal to that
predetermined rate of profit, we are at a switchpoint.

We have to be clear about what the equality of statement
(6.17) is and what it is not; for if it is looked at as:

$$\frac{\Delta y}{\Delta k} = r \qquad\qquad 6.20$$

it seems indentical to the traditional "marginal products of capital
equal to the rate of profit" concept. But there is an
essential difference in what the two equalities tell us. At
a switchpoint one can either adopt technique (A) of (B)
or some combination of the two; the level of profits is
determined by the particular stock of capital $_{or}$ combination
of stocks. The marginal product is the ratio in the limit of
the difference in two net outputs to two quantities of
capital corresponding to two techniques. In other words, the
derivitive derived this way pertains to changes in the
proportions in which two techniques are combined at the same
rate of profit. It is in this sense that the marginal product
ratio can be said to "determine" the rate of profit. Since
(r) is the same for both - as is the wage rate - it does not
enter into a determination of the change in the value of capital
as one goes from one stock (technique) to another. The change
in the quantities of this ratio must be "real" - independent
of the price effect- if it is to determine what the rate of
profit is. It is then only within the confines of a switchpoint
condition that we can talk about the marginal product as a
distributive tool in that it explains the rate of reward to
capital. Otherwise, the only way it can serve this purpose is
in the condition of the fantasy one-commodity world.

We remind ourselves that the equality of (6.20) in the neo-classical sense represents a limiting ratio of the difference in net output to that of the "quantity" of capital corresponding to two techniques, where each technique was most profitable at different rates of profit. And we have the rate of profit entering into the determinants of the increments of the ratio that is itself supposed to determine what the rate of profit is.

Now let us see what happens when we move off the switchpoint. To the left of (Q') technique (A) is more profitable at the rate of profit (r''); we can reflect this as:

$$y_B - r''k_B < y_A - r''k_A \qquad 6.21$$

$$\text{and}$$

$$\frac{y_B - y_A}{k_B - k_A} < r''$$

One technique will be more or less profitable than the other according as the profitability ratio is greater or lessor than the rate of profit. Assume that at the switchpoint technique (A) was in use, thus the same technique remains in play at a lower profit rate. What has happened is that the same capital stock has become relatively less costly at (r'') compared with technique (B); this negative price effect gives a lower value of capital and a lower level of profits due to the higher wage rate now associated with (A). In a comparison of equilibrium states, the switch from $(\bar{r}')$ to (r'') entails a lower value of capital and a lower level of profits; we find a smaller marginal product ratio that is reflective of the existence of a smaller rate of profit. But we cannot say that this smaller ratio determines the smaller rate of profit.

141

Yet this comparison of states is better appreciated if we go from a more mechanized technique (B) at the switchpoint to the less mechanized technique (A) at the changed rate of profit. Here we see the real effect in operation as the adoption of (A) results from both real and price effects; the lower (r) and higher (w) for (A) results in a profit level for (A) that exceeds the level for (B) in spite of the lower (r) and lower (w) associated with (B). But the change in the ratio of net output to value of capital is determined in part by the change in the rate of profit; and, so to speak, corresponds to it. It cannot, to reiterate, be said to explain the rate of profit.

Let us fully differentiate equation (6.10):

$$dy = rdk + kdr + dw \qquad 6.22$$

then: $dkr = -dw - kdr + dy$

and: $dk = - \{\frac{dw}{r} + \frac{k}{r}(dr)\} + \frac{dy}{r} \qquad 6.23$

When the bracketed term equals zero, we get the equality of the ratio of profitability and the rate of profit:

$$\frac{dy}{dk} = r \qquad 6.24$$

whihc is our switchpoint position. This means that the capital can be treated as a productive instrument, while it is simultaneously treated as a distributive instrument. In other words, that the stock of capital through the level of output that it gives rise to defines the distribution of between wages and profits. Should an economy become more mechanized but the rate of profit remain the same, then it can be said that the profitability ratio (the look-alike to the marginal product of capital ratio) "explains" the increase in profits; in this sense the distribution of income is defined for the existence

142

of a particular rate of profit.

The bracketed term in (6.23) represents the price
effect, which when set to zero gives:

$$-\{\frac{dw}{r} + \frac{k}{r}(dr)\} = 0 \qquad 6.25$$

and

$$k = -\frac{dw}{dr} \qquad 6.26$$

The value of capital per man is equal to the slope of the
factor-price (technique) curve; the elasticity of which at
that point gives the distribution of income. So that we
corroborate our ability to treat capital as an income bearing
property synonomous with its treatment as a factor of
production, In the switchpoint condition we have:

$$rk = -\frac{dwr}{dr} = y - w \qquad 6.27$$

and

$$k = -\frac{dw}{dr} = \frac{y - w}{r} \qquad 6.28$$

A comparison of equilibrium situations on both sides of
a switchpoint reveals differences in the value of capital per
man due to real and price effects. We get at the entire
matter by some manipulation of the totally differentiated
equation (6.10). Thus:[5]

$$\frac{dy}{dw} = 1 + \frac{dk}{dw} \cdot r + \frac{dr}{dw} \cdot k \qquad 6.29$$

then:

$$\frac{dr}{dw} \cdot k = -1 - \frac{dk}{dw} \cdot r + \frac{dy}{dw} \qquad 6.30$$

and

$$k = \{-1 - \frac{dk}{dw} \cdot r + \frac{dy}{dw}\} \cdot \frac{dw}{dy}$$

or

$$k = -\frac{dw}{dr} \{\frac{dk}{dw} \cdot r + 1 - \frac{dy}{dw}\} \qquad 6.31$$

Note that we do not get the simultaneity of the distribution and productive facets of capital unless the bracketed terms of (6.31) equal unity. Making it so gives:

$$k = - \frac{dw}{dr} \qquad\qquad 6.32$$

and as well:

$$\frac{rdk}{dw} = \frac{dy}{dw} \qquad\qquad 6.33$$

so:

$$r = \frac{dy}{dk}$$

The equality of (k) to both $- \frac{dy}{dw}$ and $\frac{y - w}{r}$ will always hold as long as the rate of profit is held constant. But the same equality via equations (6.32) and (6.33) cannot be valid in general; that is, when price effects are considered, there is no straight-away explanation for the distribution of income in terms of the marginal product of capital. This latter equality will hold, as we indicated, when we make the price effect non-operative by rendering the bracketed term of (6.31) equal to unity. By this proviso we mean that the factor-price curve for each technique is a straight line. One technique is always more profitable than another, and the distribution of income reflects the "market power" of the factor for the given productive facet of the value capital. A change in the rate of profit-wage rate relationship causes no change in the value of capital. Put it this way: if both techniques are characterized by straight lines then the difference in the value of their capital must be real at points away from the switchpoint because the price effect is neutral.

We see the point more directly via fig. (6.5).

Fig. 6.5

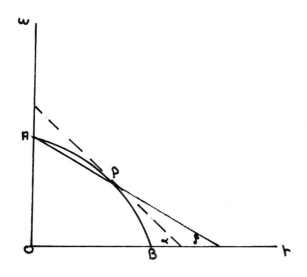

The slope of the tangent at (P), i.e. tangent (α) corresponds to the distributive facet of (k); the elasticity of the curve at that point gives the shares when factors are paid according to their marginal product. On the other hand, the output per capita given by (k) is seen with tangent (β) which is slope of line connecting points (A) and (P); the production facet being measured by the distance OA (at r = 0, y = W = OA). Now the two tangents are not equal, so that the (k) cannot explain, or be the link between the share of profits in income and the level of output attributable to the "amount" of capital.

The two tangents become equal when the wage curve is linear;

145

for the value of capital is given by the slope of the curve, and its elasticity measures income distribution.

In general, the discussion of this chapter provides a further context to house our suspicions about a marginal product explanation for relative shares. We are left with having to be at a switchpoint, or to suppose linearity of the technique curves, if we are to handle the valuation of capital. It all smacks of an amount of "real" unreality to say the least. It seems that to explain the distribution of income in an economy which, over time, alters techniques as it becomes more mechanized, one has to take the rate of profit as given from outside the system. But then what determines the rate of profit? It has been suggested that such a determination be sought within the sphere of "political economy" rather than that of technical economics.

Having to abondon neoclassical moorings, we will in the next chapter, try a different route to an explanation for the distribution of output.

NOTES

1. Taken from Joan Robinson and K. A. Naqui, "The Badly Production Function", *Quarterly Journal of Economics*, LXXXI pp. 579-91.

2. This can be demonstrated with the following relationship:

    1.55t. wheat + 2.22t. iron + .8 labor = 3,33t. wheat
    .78t. wheat + 1.11t. iron + .2 labor = 3.33t. iron

    At a rate of profit of .10, the wage rate is .60, and the value of the capital and consumption outputs are 1.59 and 3.48 respectively; with the price ratio between them being .45. At $r = 20$, $w = .20$ the capital and consumption output values are 1.65 and 3.35 respectively with the ratio between them increasing to .49.

3. Based on the work done by Luigi Spaventa, "Rate of Profit, Rate of Growth, and Capital Intensity in a Sample Production Model", *Oxford Economic Papers*, XXII, pp. 129-147.

4. This ratio is discussed in the illuminating article by D. S. Harris, "Capital, Distribution, and the Aggregate Production Function", American Economic Review, LXIII, pp. 100-113.

5. This is based on the work of A. Bhaduri, "The Concept of the Marginal Productivity of Capital and the Wicksell Effect", Oxford Economic Papers, XVIII, pp. 284-288. Also see his "On the Significance of Recent Controversies on Capital Theory : A Marxian View", *Economic Journal*, LXXIX, pp. 532-539.

7. AN ALTERNATIVE SETTING

The framework for this approach is that if full-employment is to be maintained, there is a particular amount of
investment that must be undertaken; and if it is undertaken,
there will be a particular distribution of income that provides
the savings to "support" it. Taking this ratio of investment
to output as an independent variable we can then construct a
link between the rate of profit and the distribution of income
with the rate of growth of the economy emerging from that
investment ratio. A connection is forged between the distribution
of income and capital accumulation. The rate of profit is
not treated in the "narrow" sense as a reward for the holding of
different "quantities" of capital; and as such, an explanation
for the rate of profit stands apart from the definitional
thicket of the valuation of capital. And in an overall view,
one now moves from looking at "effects", i.e. a comparison of
equilibrium positions, to that of the dynamics of steady-state
analysis.

I

We get off the ground in our new setting with the use of
Professor Kaldor's model on economic growth.[1] Kaldor's investment
function puts the inducement to invest as an increasing function
of the rate of profit and a decreasing function of the ratio
of the value of capital to that of output. In particular, the
change in the capital stock from say $(t - 1)$ to (t) is equal to
the value of investment in $(t - 1)$, but this investment is
governed by a desired level of capital in (t) which is a
function of conditions in $(t - 1)$. These conditions are the
level of output in $(t - 1)$ - relative to the existing capital
stock - and the realized rate of profit in $(t - 1)$ multiplied
by the level of output in that period. Let us take the coefficient

148

on investment of the capital/output ratio and the rate of profit as (a) and (b) respectively. At a given rate of profit, the higher the capital/output ratio the lower the desired level of capital and the lower the rate of capital accumulation.

The capital stock in (t), being the result of investment in (t - 1), can be put set down as:

$$K_t = a_{t-1} + b(r_{t-1})\, Y_{t-1} \qquad\qquad 7.1$$

Looking ahead from (t), we have:

$$I_t = K_{t+1} - K_t \qquad\qquad 7.2$$

$$= aY_t + b(r_t)Y_t - aY_{t-1} - b(r_{t-1})Y_{t-1} \qquad 7.3$$

$$=(Y_t - Y_{t-1})[a+b(r_{t-1})] + b(r_t-r_{t-1})Y_t \qquad 7.4$$

Investment in (t-1) is undertaken to adjust for the difference between an existing stock in (t-1) and what one would have liked to have had given the realized output in (t-1). So that from (7.1) we have the relationship between desired capital and output in (t-1) as:

$$\frac{K_t}{Y_{t-1}} = a + b(r_{t-1}) \qquad\qquad 7.5$$

which means that equation (7.4) can be stated as:

$$I_t=(Y_t - Y_{t-1}) \frac{K_t}{(\frac{Y}{Y_{t-1}})} + b(r_t-r_{t-1})Y_t \qquad 7.6$$

But we would like to state equation (7.6) in the form of investment as a proportion of output:[2]

$$\frac{I_t}{Y_t} = \frac{Y_t-Y_{t-1}}{Y_{t-1}} \cdot \frac{K_t}{Y_t} + b(r_t-r_{t-1}) \qquad\qquad 7.7$$

An existing rate of capital growth will be a desired rate, should the growth of output that it gives rise to be such as to fully employ it, and thereby as well, let us say, result in the full employment of the given labor force. Should the capital

149

stock in any one period be in correct relation to output as a
result of past decisions, then it can be assumed that the
existing rate of growth of capital will be desired in the future.
That is, for a given change in output, the change in capital and
thereby desired investment, will be given by the anticipated
change in output equal to the realized change (one continues
into the future the correct guess if the past) multiplied by
the capital/output ratio that one wants to maintain. For a
given rate of accumulation, there is a particular rate of
growth in output that is compatible with the economy being
willing to sustain that rate of capital growth. But all this
modified by the rate of profit; if it is falling, the economy
will put into being a lesser rate of capital accumulation at
any given capital/output ratio.

Next we need to define a savings function. Let S_W be the
savings propensity out of wages (W), and S_P be the savings
propensity out of profits (P), with the assumption $S_P > S_W$.
In this immediate discussion, the class of people called
"workers" receive income consisting entirely of wages, while
the class called "capitalists" receive all of the income
category labelled profits. No distinction need to be made
between the distribution of income between classes of income
and classes of people; but this will be modified to see what
happens when workers receive a share of total profits, which
they must if we are to presume $S_W > 0$. For now we keep S_W as a
positive term in our deliberations and tune it only to wages. Thus:

$$S_t = S_p(P_t) + S_W(Y_t - P_t)$$

$$= S_W(Y_t) + (S_P - S_W)P_t$$

7.8

And expressed as a proportion of output:

$$\frac{S_t}{Y_t} = S_P(\frac{P_t}{Y_t}) + S_W(\frac{Y_t-P_t}{Y_t})$$

$$= (S_P - S_W)\frac{P_t}{Y_t} + S_W$$

7.9

A given rate of accumulation, and thereby growth in productive capacity, gives rise to a growth in output that renders that rate of accumulation as desirable or not. If it is desirable that system will, as we indicated, undertake a similar rate of accumulation in the future to maintain the existing capital/output ratio. Now the relation between the growth of output and the rate of accumulation on which it is based is given in terms of a technical progress function. The function is stated as:

$$\frac{Y_t-Y_{t-1}}{Y_{t-1}} = n + h(\frac{I_{t-1}}{K_{t-1}})$$

7.10

or

$$\hat{Y} = n + h(\hat{K})$$

where $\hat{Y} = \frac{\dot{Y}}{Y}$, $\hat{K} = \frac{\dot{K}}{K}$

and depicted in per capita terms in fig. (7.1).

Fig. 7.1

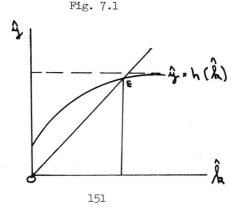

The carrier of technical progress is the physical stock of
capital. The greater its rate of accumulation, the greater
the "amount" of such progress that gets diffused into the
productive system. The level of profitable innovations goes
up in direct relation to the change in $(\hat{k})$. If one can
imagine a warehouse of ideas ready to improve per capita
output, then the rate at which these ideas can be absorbed
and exploited is itself limited by the economy's ability to
accumulate capital. Yet along this function the deepening
of capital is being carried on in a constant state of new
development; while capital per head is increasing, it is
not the same kind of capital that is being accumulated. The
convexity of the function reflects the exhaustion of new
techniques to increase productivity. There is a tapering
off to the increasing effect on $(\hat{y})$, and presumably some
upper limit no matter how fast k grows. In Kaldar's words,
". . . . the more capital is increased the more labor-paving
technical improvements can be adopted, though there is likely
to be some maximum beyond which the rate of growth in productivity
cannot be raised, however fast capital is being accumulated."[3]

The function cuts the verticle axes, therefore some increase
in productivity is possible even if the capital/labor ratio
is fixed. One can presume improvements due to organizational
changes or via "learning by doing." Also the entire function
can shift upwards due to some fundamental breakthrough - say the
ability to harness a new form of energy - that unleashes a
spate of techniques to be exploited by the accumulation of "new"
capital.

We concentrate on the condition represented by point (E)
where the capital/output ratio remains constant, but where the
capital/labor and output/labor ratios are growing at an exponential

rate. Here the rate of growth in output leaves the actual
output to capital ratio as the desired ratio which, perpetuates
the realized rate of capital accumulation and thereby the
realized pace of output growth. The actual rate of profit is
equal to the expected rate; we have a constant share of
profit in output as well as a constant proportion of investment
to output. In general, we have the economy on the steady-state
track of long-run equilibrium growth evidencing those stylized
facts that were mentioned at the end of Chapter 2.

Along this path the savings/output ratio is a constant
given the savings propensities, and its identity with the
unchanging investment/output ratio is seen by relating (7.9)
with (7.7). Thus:

$$\frac{S}{Y} = (S_P - S_W)\frac{P}{Y} + S_W = \frac{I}{Y} \qquad 7.11$$

and

$$\frac{P}{Y} = \frac{1}{S_P - S_W}\left(\frac{I}{Y}\right) - \frac{S_W}{S_P - S_W} \qquad 7.12$$

The equilibrium condition is supported by a particular ratio
of profits to income; this distribution of income gives rise to
a rare of savings that is equal to the rate of investment induced
by this ratio. The unchanging rate of profit which gives this
constant ratio of profits to income for the given capital to
output ratio, can be determined from equation (7.12). As the
rate of profit (r) is:

$$r = \frac{P}{Y} \cdot \frac{Y}{K} \qquad 7.13$$

then:

$$r = \frac{P}{Y} \cdot \frac{Y}{K} = \left[\frac{1}{S_P - S_W}\left(\frac{I}{Y}\right) - \frac{S_W}{S_P - S_W}\right]\frac{Y}{K} \qquad 7.14$$

however, from (7.7) we now have:

153

$$\frac{I}{Y} = \frac{Y_t - Y_{t-1}}{Y_{t-1}} \cdot \frac{K}{Y} \qquad\qquad 7.15$$

then:

$$r = [\frac{1}{S_P - S_W} (\hat{Y} \cdot \frac{K}{Y}) - \frac{S_W}{S_P - S_W}]\frac{Y}{K} \qquad 7.16$$

but:

$$\hat{Y} \cdot \frac{K}{Y} = \hat{Y}/\frac{Y}{K}, \text{ hence:}$$

$$r = \frac{1}{S_P - S_W}(\hat{Y}) - (\frac{S_W}{S_P - S_W})\frac{Y}{K} \qquad 7.17$$

The determinants of the rate of profit (given the savings propensities) are the rate of growth in output and the output of capital ratio. Let us designate the equality of the growth rates of capital and output (on a per capita basis) in this equilibrium state by the symbol (g). Now if we take $S_W=0$ (this is what Kaldor must have had in mind by his construction that workers receive no part of profits, but even if it were positive, it was assumed to be insignificant and play no role in determining the long-run outcome) then the distribution of income is given by:

$$\frac{P}{Y} = \frac{1}{S_P}(\frac{I}{Y}) \qquad\qquad 7.18$$

And the rate of profit is:

$$r = \frac{g}{S_P} \qquad\qquad 7.19$$

The idea of the investment to output ratio as an independent variable must be seen with regard to the state that the economy is in. As we do assume the steady-state condition, then by definition the ratio is determined and a constant; the task then is to understand the balances required to keep the economy on the path. Furthermore is we say $S_W=0$, $S=1$, then $S=P=I$; the earnings of capitalist's (i.e. profits) are equal to the sum of investments, and these earninigs are all again invested (neglecting capitalist's

154

consumption). Along the path, the ratio of investment to income yields a particular ratio of profits to income, such that the level of savings is always appropriate to that level of investment needed to maintain the particular growth rate.

Let us set out the ingredients in the following order:

    a.   Saving function

$$\frac{S}{Y} = S_p \left(\frac{P}{Y}\right) \qquad\qquad 7.20$$

    b.   Investment function.

$$\frac{I}{Y} = g\left(\frac{K}{Y}\right) \qquad\qquad 7.21$$

    c.   The equality along the path being maintained by a particular profit share is income.

$$\frac{S}{Y} = \frac{I}{Y} \qquad\qquad 7.22$$

    d.   Then:

$$S_p \left(\frac{P}{Y}\right) = g\left(\frac{K}{Y}\right)$$

$$\text{and } \frac{P}{Y} = \frac{1}{S_p} \left[g\left(\frac{K}{Y}\right)\right] \qquad\qquad 7.23$$

with $S_p = 1$:

$$\frac{P}{Y} = g\left(\frac{K}{Y}\right) \qquad\qquad 7.24$$

$$\text{also: } r = \frac{1}{S_p} (g) \qquad\qquad 7.25$$

In fig. (7.2) we see the savings and investment functions plotted against the profit share.

Fig. 7.2

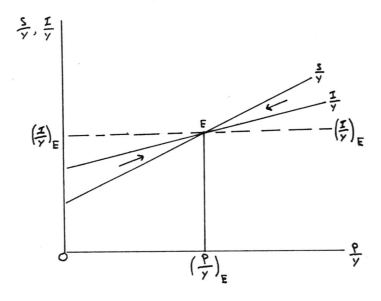

Keeping with the form of the model where $S_W > 0$, we have the savings function at the verticle axis; but with $S_W = 0$, the function begins at the origin, and where $S_p = 1$, it is the $45°$ line. The investment function is determined for the particulars of the steady-state condition, and should supposedly be drawn with a zero slope; thus for a system in equilibrium the stability for it comes through adjustments in the savings function. But in fig. (7.2) the investment function is upward sloping, we can then talk about adjustments along both functions to the position

156

of the steady-state (E), where the analysis is then in terms
of the given $(\frac{I}{Y})_E$.

For a share of profits to the left of (E), we find that
the level of investment that it stimulates exceeds the level
of savings appropriate to it given the savings propensities.
The demand conditions causes prises to rise relative to wages
with the consequent increase in profit margins and the profit
share. As we can see from equation (7.7), an increase in
the rate of profit stimulates an increase in the investment
ratio that exceeds the realized rate of growth in output.
But this higher profit share begets as well a greater rate of
increase in the share of savings, which lessens the increase
to profit margins, and thereby the rate of further stimulation
to investment and employment. In the move to the full-employment
position at (E), it is the variation in investment associated
with the shift in the distribution to profits that accounts
for changes in output and employment.

The system does not get stuck at a point below (E) as
long as we assume that the balance between savings and
investment is achievable in the relationship between prices and
costs. We have the usual Keynesian interpretation of events,
but one step removed. Both savings and investment are functionally
related to output change, but where the growth in output is
itself hinged to income distribution. The rate of growth in
output is increasing as long as I/Y>S/Y mirroring the increase
in the share of profits in output. Thus the multiplier-accelerator
mechanism can explain output and employment changes as well as
variations in distribution as long as the economy is not
operating in its long-run equilibrium position. But once the
economy is positioned in the steady-state condition full-employment
is assured and the rate of output growth is given. The level of

157

aggregate output is always appropriate to the full-employment
condition; the stability of this condition is then given in
terms of the distribution of this output, rather than through
variations in its level (this latter relationship holding in the
strict Keynesian circumstance of underemployment equilibrium).[4]

We get a clear notion of this by viewing fig. (7.2) with
the investment ratio as a horizontal straight line. From
a point to the left of (E), planned savings as it relates
to the particular income distribution, results in excess
demand raising price and profits. But note that $d(\frac{I}{Y}) = 0$,
so that we are dealing with a change in the distribution of
an aggregate output growing at some constant rate. While on
the other side, planned savings in relation to the given
share of investment results in excess supply pressures. This
now shows up in the form of downward prices and shares of
profits in income; the associated decline in planned savings
continuing until the excess supply is removed. The point to
bear in mind, is that within this framework the decline in
demand is met with a reduction in profits, and not with a
reduction in investment and employment.

But this kind of adjustment via an increase in the real
wage does assume that the profit share, in the aggregate, is
above some necessary minimum, if this approach is a reasonable
explanation of stability. And from the left of (E) it is
assumed that the decline in the real wage will be "allowed"
to occur in response to excess demand; otherwise, the insufficient
shift to profits could disintegrate the necessary level of the
investment share. And, in the move to the steady-state, the
system will fall short of that point if profit share flexibility
is aborted.

II

A necessary adjustment of Kaldor's savings function is

158

provided by Pasinetti's reformulation of the model.[5] As we
have seen, the savings function assumes that the workers do
save, but do solely out of an income category called wages.
Yet if workers save, they do not transfer these savings as a
gift to capitalists, nor are these savings confiscated and
ownership of them transferred to capitalists. Certainly
if workers were not permitted to own their savings, and to
receive a reward for its accumulation, then what is the
incentive for not consuming all?   If workers as a class
of people are not to be presumed to follow that attribute
normally assigned to them, namely, to spend all that they
earn, they have to be rewarded for transferring part of
their income to the class called capitalists whose role is
to invest and generate income. The payment to workers
for this transfer (via intermediary agencies) is made by
capitalists from there income, i.e. from profits. The
fact that workers have saved means that they own part of
the capital stock (indirectly, through loans of "financial
capital" to capitalists), and will therefore receive a part
of the total profits generated by this capital.

The savings function will have to be restated to account
for the distinction between categories of income (profits and
wages) and the distribution of this income between categories
of people (capitalists and workers). Of course, if we assume
that there is no savings out of wages, the two concepts become
identical. Letting (π) stand for capitalists and (O) for workers
[to distinguish it now from wages (W)], we write the savings
function as:

$$S = S_O(Y - P_O - P_\pi + P_O) + S_\pi(P_\pi)$$
$$= S_O(Y + P_\pi) + S_\pi(P_\pi) \qquad\qquad 7.26$$
$$S = S_O(Y) + (S_\pi - S_O)P_\pi$$

In equilibrium:

$$\frac{S}{Y} = \frac{I}{Y} \qquad\qquad 7.27$$

then: $\quad S_O + \dfrac{(S_\pi - S_O)P_\pi}{Y} = \dfrac{I}{Y}$

and: $\quad \dfrac{P_\pi}{Y} = \dfrac{1}{S_\pi - S_O}\left(\dfrac{I}{Y}\right) - \dfrac{S_O}{S_\pi - S_O} \qquad\qquad 7.28$

But this equilibrium statement does not give a true picutre of that requisite income distribution, all it shows is that part of profits which accrues to the capitalists. In order to see the ratio of total profits to income, we need to add the share of workers' profits to equation (7.28).

But before we do this, let us extract the equilibrium rate of profits under the new savings function. Thus:

$$S_O\left(\frac{Y}{K}\right) + (S_\pi - S_O)\frac{P_\pi}{K} = \frac{I}{K} \qquad\qquad 7.29$$

and: $\quad (S_\pi - S_O)\dfrac{P_\pi}{K} = \dfrac{I}{K} - S_O\left(\dfrac{Y}{K}\right)$

then: $\quad \dfrac{P_\pi}{K} = \dfrac{1}{S_\pi - S_O}\left(\dfrac{I}{K}\right) - \dfrac{S_O}{S_\pi - S_O}\left(\dfrac{Y}{K}\right) \qquad\qquad 7.30$

Expression (7.30), as well, presents a limited picture, for it gives the ratio of part of total profits to total capital. A true expression for the rate of profit requires that we add the

160

ratio $\frac{P_O}{K}$ to both sides of (7.30).

To find the equilibrium expressions for the rate of profit and the distribution of income, we need to alter equations (7.28) and (7.30) to reflect the fact that:

$$\frac{P}{Y} = \frac{P_\pi}{Y} + \frac{P_O}{Y}$$

$$r \equiv \frac{P}{K} = \frac{P_\pi}{K} + \frac{P_O}{K} \qquad 7.31$$

We start with the rate of profit.

We add the term $\frac{P_O}{K} \equiv \frac{rK_O}{K}$ to both side of (7.30). The ratio of capital owned by workers (indirectly) to the total stock of capital is:

$$\frac{K_O}{K} = \frac{S_O}{S} = \frac{S_O(Y-P_\pi)}{I} \qquad 7.32$$

And from the steady-state equilibrium of I=S, we obtain an expression for $\frac{P_\pi}{I}$ as:

$$\frac{P_\pi}{I} = \frac{I}{S_\pi - S_O}(1 - S_O \cdot \frac{Y}{I}) \qquad 7.33$$

Then:
$$\frac{K_O}{K} = S_O \left[\frac{Y}{I} - \frac{1}{S_\pi - S_O}(1 - S_O \cdot \frac{Y}{I})\right] \qquad 7.34$$

$$= S_O \left[\frac{Y}{I} + \frac{S_O}{S_\pi - S_O} \cdot \frac{Y}{I} - \frac{1}{S_\pi - S_O}\right] \qquad 7.35$$

$$= \left(\frac{S_O^2}{S_\pi - S_O} + S_O\right)\frac{Y}{I} - \frac{S_O}{S_\pi - S_O} \qquad 7.36$$

$$= \frac{S_\pi S_O}{S_\pi - S_O} \cdot \frac{Y}{I} - \frac{S_O}{S_\pi - S_O} \qquad 7.37$$

161

By adding (7.37) to (7.30), and writing $\frac{P}{K}$ for r, we obtain a total rate of profit statement. Thus:

$$\frac{P}{K} = \frac{1}{S_\pi - S_0} \cdot \frac{I}{K} - \frac{S_0}{S_\pi - S_0} \cdot \frac{Y}{K} + \frac{P}{K}(\frac{S_\pi S_0}{S_\pi - S_0} \cdot \frac{Y}{I} - \frac{S_0}{S_\pi - S_0}) \quad 7.38$$

and: $\frac{P}{K}(1 - \frac{S_\pi S_0}{S_\pi - S_0} \cdot \frac{Y}{I} + \frac{S_0}{S_\pi - S_0}) = \frac{1}{S_\pi - S_0} \cdot \frac{I}{K} - \frac{S_0}{S_\pi - S_0} \cdot \frac{Y}{K} \quad 7.39$

then: $\frac{P}{K}[\frac{(S_\pi - S_0)I - (S_\pi S_0)Y + S_0 I}{(S_\pi - S_0)I}] = \frac{I - S_0(Y)}{(S_\pi - S_0)K} \quad 7.40$

leading to: $\frac{P}{K}[\frac{S_\pi I - (S_\pi S_0)Y}{I}] = \frac{I - S_0(Y)}{K}$

$$\frac{P}{K} \cdot S_\pi \frac{I - S_0(Y)}{I} = \frac{I - S_0(Y)}{K} \quad 7.41$$

On the assumption that $I - S_0(Y) > 0$, then:

$$\frac{P}{K} \cdot \frac{S_\pi}{I} \cdot I - S_0(Y) = \frac{1}{K} \cdot I - S_0(Y) \quad 7.42$$

and: $\frac{P}{K} \cdot \frac{S_\pi}{I} = \frac{1}{K}$

$$\frac{P}{K} = \frac{1}{S_\pi} \cdot \frac{I}{K} \quad 7.43$$

To adjust equation (7.28) we add $\frac{P_0}{Y}$ to both sides. This ratio of workers' profits to income is equal to (via equation 7.37):

$$r[\frac{S_\pi S_0}{S_\pi - S_0} \cdot \frac{K}{I} - \frac{S_0}{S_\pi - S_0} \cdot \frac{K}{Y}] \quad 7.44$$

Then:

$$\frac{P}{Y} = \frac{1}{S_\pi - S_0} \cdot \frac{I}{Y} - \frac{S_0}{S_\pi - S_0} + r[\frac{S_\pi S_0}{S_\pi - S_0} \cdot \frac{K}{I} - \frac{S_0}{S_\pi - S_0} \cdot \frac{K}{Y}] \quad 7.45$$

leading to: $\frac{P}{Y} = \frac{1}{S_\pi} \cdot \frac{I}{Y} \quad 7.46$

The end-all of this adjustment is an understanding that
while the workers' propensity to save does determine the share
of profits that accrues to them (through equation 7.28), and
hence determines the distribution of income between them and
capitalists; it does not determine the aggregate level of
profits. The act of savings by workers does not influce the
distribution of income level as between total profits and total
wages (as we see via equation 7.46), but, to reiterate, it does
influence the distribution of that given income level as between
"classes of people." And as we see via equation 7.43), it would
as well have no effect on the rate of profit. The characteristics
of the economy in long-run equilibrium are those which were
worked out previously in equations (7.20 - 7.25), but now
without the uncomfortable supposition of $S_0 = 0$.

A particular ratio of aggreagte profits to income underpins
the long run path; and these profits are distributed amongst the
workers and capitalists in proportion to the amount of savings
each class contributes i.e. in proportion to the amount of capital
each owns, since for either group the ownership of capital is
rewarded at the same rate.

We write:

$$\frac{P_\pi}{S_\pi} = \frac{P_0}{S_0}$$

or

$$\frac{P_\pi}{S_\pi(P_\pi)} = \frac{P_0}{S_0(W+P_0)}$$

7.47

Note that the workers' propensity to save is the same out of wage
income as out of profit income, thefact that workers realize
profits as part of their income does not effect the proportion of

163

their income saved. This adjustment does not alter the aggregate savings ratio, and hence the ratio of investment to income.

Workers do save out of profits they receive at a lessor rate than capitalists would have saved had these profits been retained by them. But this lower rate (higher consumption out of profits) is offset by the addition of savings out of wages in the same proportion. Therefore, the aggregate savings ratio for the economy as a whole is unchanged; for $S_O(W+P_O)$ is the same as $S_\pi(P_O)$.

We see this by manipulating equation (7.47) to read:

$$S_O(W + P_O) = S_\pi(P_O) \qquad 7.48$$

When workers save, they must receive enough profits such as to make their total savings equal to what it would have been had the capitalists kept these profits and saved them at their higher rate.

Or we can write:

$$S_O(W) = [(1-S_O) - (1-S_\pi)]P_O \qquad 7.49$$

which is, as we just mentioned, that workers savings out of wage income offsets their higher level of consumption out of profits, as compared to what capitalists would have consumed out of these profits had they retained them.

The point of this is that workers share in a profit pool that is determined for them; since their act of saving will have no effect on the total amount invested and thereby on the ratio of profits to income. The capitalist's savings consists of his own, plus what he borrows from workers; which, upon investment, yields a level of income (profits) to him which is in some proportion shared with workers. Of course, workers can enlargen their share of whatever profits are generated by deciding to lend

164

a greater proportion of their income. But we remind ourselves
of the proviso that workers savings are not to equal or
exceed the total investment undertaken by the economy. This
brings up other possibilities that we liik at further along.

III

Our "alternative setting" is one where the rate of profit
is determined by the rate of growth of the economy and the
marginal propensity to save of the capitalist; and that the
rate of growth depends upon the growth of technical progress
and that of the labor force. We find no reference in this
(neo-Keynesian) approach to a "marginal productivity principle."
Or, are we somehow overlooking its presence.

Let us take another look at the equilibrium path, and restate
the distribution condition.

$$\frac{P}{Y} = \frac{1}{S_\pi} \left(\frac{I}{K} \cdot \frac{K}{Y} \right) \qquad\qquad 7.50$$

The supportive ratio of $\frac{P}{Y}$ is determined for a given ratio of
capital to output. In other words, the steady-state rate of
profit is one which is maximum for this technique $(\frac{K}{Y})$ at the
existing wage-price relationship. The stability of the path
assumes that $(\frac{K}{Y})$ is unchanging as profit margins are altered via
price flexibility. But what if a fall in the ratio of profits to
output, for example, is responded to by the introduction of more
labor-saving techniques; that is, increasing $(\frac{K}{Y})$ and thus $(\frac{I}{Y})$, with
the effect of increasing $(\frac{P}{Y})$. The ratio of $(\frac{P}{Y})$ can be said to be
determined for a given $(\frac{K}{Y})$ only in its steady-state condition, but if
the distribution ratio is falling, the capital ratio will be rising
and a new steady-state condition will emerge that reflects a higher
ratio of capital to output and a higher ratio of profits to output.
On this path the system is again proceeding steadily, but with a
higher capital to labor ratio. In this framework, the sensitivity

of $(\frac{K}{Y})$ to a change in $(\frac{P}{Y})$ is more telling than the change
in the ratio of savings to output; thus the technology changes
before market conditions restores the proper income distribution
at the original technique. We may have a sort of marginal
productivity notion, in that the equilibrium path investment
to output ratio is not independent of the rate of profit that
is associated with it. The rate of profit does play an underlining
role to the growth path, in that given the capital to output
ratio, it ensures the proper level of effective demand to
sustain it.

Pasinetti gets out of the neo-classical snare of the
intertwining between the rate of profit and the optimum
technique of production, by holding to the following causal
chain. "The externally given rate of population growth and
the capitalists' propensity to save determine first of all the
rate of profit. At this rate of profit, the optimum technique
is chosen (in such a way as to satisfy the marginal productivity
conditions.) Then, the optimum technique, together with the
rate of population growth, uniquely determine the equilibrium
investment-income ratio."[6] The capital-output ratio may be determined for a rate of profit, but it does not itself determine
what that rate will be.

We can use the following set of equations to zero in on the
essential difference between the neo-Keynesian and neo-classical
views.

$$Y = F\ (L,\ K) \qquad\qquad 7.51$$

$$w = \frac{dY}{dL},\ r = \frac{dY}{dK} \qquad\qquad 7.52$$

$$Y = P + W \qquad\qquad 7.53$$

$$I = S \qquad\qquad 7.54$$

$$I = I^* \qquad\qquad 7.55$$

What is characteristic of the neo-classical view is that
investment is not an arbitrary given (I)* but is adjusted to
planned savings through some mechanism outside the system. For
example, via flexible interest rates through monetary action,
or by some pattern of government action. On the other hand, the
neo-Keynesian would hold to a model consisting of equations
(7.51, 7.53, 7.54, 7.55); eschewing any marginal product explanation of income shares, and allowing changes in shares (resulting
from the impact of excess demand or excess supply on flexible
prices) to adjust savings to an arbitrary investment level - perhaps
determined by the expected rate of growth of output. While the
rate of interest does not adjust investment to savings; it is,
for the neo-Keynesians, the mechanism that adjusts savings to
investment. Both school of thought accord the rate of profit (rate
of interest) the role of balancing agent that secures the
full-employment growth path.

IV

The Thrust of Pasinetti's adjustment of the Kaldor model can
be said to be the irrelevancy of workers' propensity to save
within the confines of $S_\pi > S_O$. This means that while workers'
savings are always a part of total investment, the growth of
their savings will not yield them the total ownership of wealth,
so that they end up doing all the accumulation. The ratio of
investment to output that is necessary to maintain the growth
path is greater than the savings on the part of those who
both work and own capital. We have the condition:

$$S_O < \frac{I}{Y}$$

or   7.56

$$S_O < S_\pi(\frac{P}{Y})$$

167

The question is, what is the value to the upper limit of (S_0) before it reverses condition (7.56), and the full-employment path breaks down due to insufficiency of demand. We need to keep in mind that even if capitalists as a class were to disappear, and the society composed only of a "community of workers," this community would suffer underemployment if it insists on saving more than the required total investment. Now in the two class society, there would be some level of (S_0) that would yield "excessive" aggregate savings, but as we will see, in the event of this the two class notion breaks down, and we end up with only one class of savers, namely the workers. So that at some point, the savings propensity of workers (now that of society) does matter with regard to its compatibility with the steady-state full-employment path.

Professors Samuelson and Modigliani (S-M) set up a neo-classical formulation of the Pasinetti-Kaldor model;[7] and they demonstrate that for the savings propensity of workers to be irrelevant, it needs to be equal to or less than 0.05. This requirement is certainly more restrictive than Pasinetti's which was merely that the savings of workers be less than that of capitalists [the condition in equation (7.56)]. If we let $S_\pi = 1$, then the path is set out solely in terms of the capitalist's saving activity. But if we allow workers to share in the saving activity, then we can set $S_\pi < 1$ by the amount that S_0 rises above zero; yet the aggregate level of savings as a proportion of income will not grow as a result of workers acquiring some share of total profits. The Pasinetti version is that the savings ratio will become excessive if workers save out of profits alone more than capitalists would have saved out of them, and thus when we add workers' savings out of their wages to what they save out of their profits it would certainly

168

lead to too little demand, with a subsequent output growth
below the full-employment rate. S-M show that not only must
the savings propensity of workers meet the general condition
of equation (7.56) if the steady-state is to hold, but it
must be less than a rather low rate.

Let us see part of their analysis. With the labor force
growing at a rate (λ), the growth in capital owned by capitalists
on a per unit labor basis is:

$$\hat{k}_\pi = \frac{\dot{k}_\pi}{k_\pi} = \frac{S_\pi(P_\pi)}{K_\pi} - \lambda \qquad 7.57$$

and that for workers is:

$$\hat{k}_O = \frac{\dot{k}_O}{K_O} = \frac{S_O(Y-P+P_O)}{K_O} - \lambda \qquad 7.58$$

Using the marginal productivity "explanations" of equation (7.52),
and substituting into equation (7.57) and (7.58) gives:

$$\hat{k}_\pi = \frac{S_\pi[f'(k)k_\pi]}{K_\pi} - \lambda \qquad 7.59$$

$$= S_\pi[f'(k)] - \lambda \qquad 7.60$$

$$\text{and} \quad \hat{k}_O = \frac{S_O[f(k)-k_\pi f'(k)]}{K_O} \qquad 7.61$$

Along the equilibrium path (designated by *) we have $\dot{k}_\pi=0$, $\dot{k}_O=0$,
then from (7.60):

$$S_\pi[f')k^*)] - \lambda = 0$$
$$\text{and} \qquad\qquad\qquad 7.62$$
$$f'(k^*) = r^* = \frac{\lambda}{S_\pi}$$

where the growth rate of output equals that of the labor force. Along the path we find output, consumption and capital all growing exponentially at the λ rate - which is a measure of the growth of the labor force in efficiency units.

Stating equation (7.61) in terms of $\dot{k}_0$, we have:

$$\dot{k}_0 = [S_0(f(k) - f'(k)k) + s_0 f'(k)k_0] - \lambda \qquad 7.63$$

If $k_0 = 0$, then $\dot{k}_0 = 0$ since workers must own part of the capital if they are to save at all. Then $k_0 = 0$ means $S_0 = 0$, and $s_\pi = 1$. The steady-state condition equation (7.62) become $r^* = \lambda$. The growth path is given for the condition $k_0 \overset{=}{>} 0$.

The ratio of the steady-state values of k_π and k_0 is:

$$\frac{k_\pi^*}{k_0^*} = \frac{S_\pi(\frac{P}{Y}) - S_0}{S_0(\frac{W}{Y})} \qquad 7.64$$

To show the positive value of the numerator of (7.64) - the condition of equation (7.56) - we state it as:

$$\frac{P}{Y} = \frac{(rk)^*}{f(k^*)}, \quad r = \frac{\lambda}{S_\pi} \qquad 7.65$$

and:

$$\frac{S_\pi[\lambda(\frac{k^*}{S_\pi})]}{f(k^*)} = \lambda[\frac{k^*}{f(k^*)}] \qquad 7.66$$

then:

$$k_\pi^* > 0 \text{ when } S_0 < \lambda [\frac{k^*}{f(k^*)}] \qquad 7.67$$

The stringency of condition (7.67) is seen from the fact that the capital share is "generally" less than one, and empirically very much **less** than one."[8] Taking the S-M values of $\frac{P}{Y}$ = .25 and S_π = .20, the value of S_0 cannot exceed .05 if the aggregate savings behavior of the workers is to remain irrelevant.[9]

In line with neo-classical expression, we restate the investment ratio:

$$\frac{I}{K} = \lambda\left[\frac{k^*}{f(k^*)}\right] \qquad 7.68$$

$$(g = \lambda)$$

and we get at a further dimension, that of the type of production function, in the determination of the steady-state outcome. Before considering this, we look further at the limiting condition of (7.67). Assuming that S_π and λ are given, then positive values of S_0 will (within the confines of 7.67) have no effect on the equilibrium solution in terms of (r) and (k). Of course, capital owned by capitalists as a proportion of output will be diminished as a result of a rising propensity to save by workers, but as long as S_0 is sufficiently small there is no lasting increase in per capita wealth.

The fact of $S_0 > 0$, will cause capital to rise in excess of its steady-state level given for the initial condition $S_0 = 0$. Now the effect of this is to cause, in the short term that $y > y^*$; but also that $r < r^*$, which itself reduces the rate at which capitalists are accumulating capital, and which in turn reduces the rate of growth in output per head - pulling it back to its equilibrium level - so that when k_π fall to the level reflective of $y = y^*$, we have that workers are accumulating capital equal to the difference between k^* and k_π^*.

Thus for higher values of S_0, the k_π^* becomes a smaller portion of k^*; and the aggregate level of savings and accumulation of capital does not become excessive. But upon $S_0 = .05$, the idea of the two classes in the society with their particular "raison d'etre" comes to an end. The class of people called workers

(now capitalists?) end up doing all the accumulation and owning
all of the total wealth. We end up with one category of savers;
the equilibrium path does not break down it is carried on under the
condition that:

$$S_0 = \frac{I}{Y} = \lambda\left[\frac{k^*}{F(k^*)}\right]$$ 7.69

There emerges a community in which there is no place for
capitalists; where the responsibility for carrying on the
production process and the direct ownership of all means of
production are taken over by the state. Now that part of total
output that is not paid out to individuals in the form of wages
plus interest on loans made to the state previously, is labelled
as state "profits" or savings. In this context the state is the
capitalist with a propensity to save equal to unity. We have:

$$\frac{P}{Y} = \frac{I}{Y}$$ 7.70

$$\frac{P}{K} = \frac{I}{K} = \lambda$$

it is like the two class society with the assumption $S_0 = 0$.

But it should be stressed that each individual in this workers
society may decide for himself what part of this total income he
wants to lend to the state. But once it is lent, the state
then invests all; the resultant income of which is then
distributed to wages plus interest and state profits. Thus we
can say that that part of output not kept (saved) by the state is,
so to speak, consumed by it [i.e. distributed to individuals];
and that part which is kept is entirely invested. Investment though
is not only limited to profits as such; it includes a portion of the
state's distribution that flows back to it and which is then added
to state profits. The savings propensity on the part of individuals
determines what part of output is labeled "profits" and thus goes to
make up the totality of investment. Can such a community (workers plus t

172

state) maintain equilibrium growth by continuously generating
the proper lend of savings? Or, is it prone to under-investment
and disguised unemployment.

Where workers' savings do not matter the equilibrium path
is determined by the condition (in the neo-classical frame)
that the marginal product of capital must be equal to the ratio
$\frac{\lambda}{S_\pi}$; and on the other side, where workers savings do matter − it is the

only savings − the path is given by the condition that the
average product of capital must be equal to $\frac{\lambda}{S_0}$. It is this

latter regime that S-M refer to as their duality theorem; and it
has been labeled by Kaldor as the anti-Pasinetti theorem.

Pasinetti points out that this dual regime − triggered when
S_0 reaches a modest 5% − is based upon some unreasonable numbers.[10]
The S-M numbers for $\frac{P}{Y}$ and S_π means a value of $\frac{I}{Y}$ of 5%; and if we
presume a secular growth rate of 4%, then $\frac{I}{K}$ = 4%, and this implies
a $\frac{K}{Y}$ of 1.25. Working this backward to the profit share we have:

$$\frac{P}{Y} = \frac{1}{.20}(.04 + 1.25) = .25 \qquad 7.71$$

and S_0 must not exceed 5%. But if we take a more realistic number
for the capital to output ratio of 3.5 and a growth rate of 4% while
keeping the S-M value of S_π = .20, the profit share comes to:

$$\frac{P}{Y} = \frac{1}{.20}(.04 + 3.5) = 0.7 \qquad 7.72$$

implying an investment to income ratio of 14%. The value of S_0
which would be needed to bring on the dual is now 14%, which,
to quote Pasinetti, "seems to me far beyond workers saving propensity
either at present or in the foreseeible future."[11] The Pasinetti
treatment of workers savings in the equilibrium condition is then

not severely restricted in its generality; the workers propensity from being greater than zero to a level of 14% would seem to cover all realistic ground.

A recent look at the long-run average values of the capital/output and wage/income ratios was undertaken by Professor Helmstadter.[12] His data for Germany at three observations are:

Year	$\frac{K}{Y}$	$\frac{I}{K}$	$\frac{W}{Y}$
1850	5.1	.051	.74
1874	4.8	.048	.77
1913	5.4	.056	.70

We get an average growth of capital of .051, which we can take as an approximation of the equilibrium value, and we also get an average value for $\frac{K}{Y}$ of 5.1. These numbers imply a long run investment to income ratio of .26 which corresponds to the average ratio of profits to income. We have an outcome on the assumption that $S_\pi = 1$. But this value for $\frac{I}{Y}$ is too high because non-wage income is in reality not all invested. Thus if we lower the capital accumulation rate to .04 while maintaining the average value for the capital to output ratio and profit share, we get a ratio of $\frac{I}{Y} = .20$ that corresponds to $S_\pi = .77$. Based on these numbers, workers' savings would not matter as long as $S_0 < .20$.

V

Whether the equilibrium path is characterized by the Pasinetti condition or by its dual depends on the interplay of the savings propensities, the rate of growth along the path and, what we want to get at in this section, the technical considerations of production.

174

To being with, we look at Pasinetti's own claim that his conclusions regarding the long run rate of profit is independent of any assumption about whether and how technology (in the sense of the capital-output ratio) is influenced by changes in the rate of profit." Within the realm of S_0 continuing to satisfy equation (7.56), the steady-state rate of profit is independent of the production function; there is no presumption of any particular technique of production.

Picking up with the rate of profit equation (7.43) which we repeat here:

$$r \equiv \frac{P}{K} = \frac{1}{S_\pi} \cdot \frac{I}{K} \qquad 7.73$$

$$\text{then:} \quad S_\pi(rk) = I$$

and stating this with the use of the traditional (Cobb-Douglas) production function, we have:

$$S_\pi[F(K,L) - W] = I \qquad 7.74$$

as $K = k, L$ then:

$$I = \frac{dK}{dt} = \frac{kdL}{dt} + \frac{Ldk}{dt}$$

$$= k\lambda L + \frac{Ldk}{dt} \qquad 7.75$$

But along the equilibrium path $\frac{dk}{dt} = 0$, so that:

$$S_\pi(rK) = k\lambda L$$

$$\text{or}$$

$$S_\pi(rK) = K\lambda \qquad 7.76$$

$$\text{and:}$$

$$S_\pi(r) = \lambda$$

$$\text{or}$$

$$r = \frac{\lambda}{S_\pi} \qquad 7.77$$

175

The basic Pasinetti expression for the rate of profit is confirmed even if we presumed that the economy could elect any one of an "infinite" number of capital to labor ratios.

We remind ourselves that if the Cobb-Douglas rules, then the distribution of income is given by the function; that is, a change in technique has no effect on the ratio of profits to income. Thus, with income shares given, the equilibrium technique (the capital to output ratio) cannot be determined by it; the technique is determined by the exogoneous forces of the ratio of the aggregate propensity to save to the growth of the effective labor force. This technique, in turn, determines the equilibrium ratio of investment to output.

We can run the causal chain in the following direction. The rate of profit is determined by the forces of the ratio in equation (7.77); and this $(r*)$ mirrors the being of a technique of production that maintains the steady-state condition. In this sense the technique is optimum; in that it requires a particular ratio of investment to output such that it leads to the equality of the growth rates of effective labor, output and capital. What the introduction of the conventional function does is to show sufficient flexibility in the technique of production; the capital to output ratio will adopt to the independently determined rate of profit. The steady-state condition that we talk about may, of course, be unachievable; but not on account of a constancy of the technical framework. We also reiterate that in this Pasinetti (Neo-Keynesian) world there is the co-determination of the ratio of profits to income and the rate of profit, both flowing from the relation of the savings propensity and the steady-state growth rate.

We make use of a diagrammatic analysis to help us see the long-run equilibrium outcomes.[13] There is the possibility that no such outcome is possible, due to either savings or technological

176

difficulties. There is the neo-Keynesian outcome in which
the savings propensity of capitalists matter only, and where
the path is characterized by the condition $\frac{P}{K} = \frac{\lambda}{S_\pi}$. In this
state the ownership of capital is divided in some proportion
between the two classes. And there is the possibility of the
anti-Pasinetti outcome, in which workers and up doing all the
accumulation, and the distribution of the capital settles at a
value where $\frac{Y}{K} = \frac{\lambda}{S_0}$.

In this last (dual) case we find savings proportional to
income (not profits), and the equilibrium outcome does depend
on a particular ratio of output to capital. Thus:

$$\frac{I}{K} = S_0 (\frac{Y}{K}) = \lambda$$

$$\text{and} \qquad\qquad\qquad 7.78$$

$$\frac{Y}{K} = \frac{\lambda}{S_0}$$

In order to solve for the rate of profit, one has to solve for
the technological aspects of the growth condition; i.e. to know
what the capital to output ratio is. That is:

$$r = \frac{P}{Y} \cdot \frac{Y}{K}$$

$$\text{and} \qquad\qquad\qquad 7.79$$

$$r = \frac{\frac{P}{Y}}{S_0} (\lambda)$$

Once the growth rate is given, and this is not independent of the
form of the production function, the rate of profit is then determined
by the ratio of the profit share to the workers' savings propensity.

In a world where workers (being the only class of people)
receive both classes of income, the distribution of income will

effect total savings and thereby the rate of profit. Workers
(the state?) would determine into which category they throw
what part of income. But in the two classes of people world,
the earnings of one class automatically determines the proportion of profits to income; thus the determination of the rate
of profit does not have to depend upon an explicit consideration
of the distribution of income.

Fig. (7.3) lays out the boundaries that designate the
steady-state outcomes.

Fig. 7.3

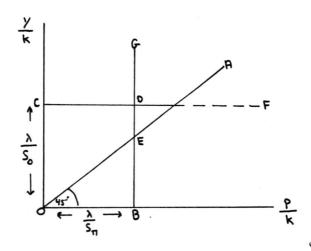

A point on the 45° line such as E shows $\frac{Y}{K} = \frac{P}{K}$, telling us that
profits absorbs the whole of the national income; and a point
in the space below OA shows $\frac{P}{K} > \frac{Y}{K}$, i.e profits would absorb more
than the whole of output. We are then only concerned with the
economically meaningful upper portion of the quadrant between OA

178

and the vertical axis.

The segment OB gives the ratio $\frac{\lambda}{S_\pi}$, and the segment OC is equal to the ratio of the dual outcome $\frac{\lambda}{S_O}$; the length of the latter exceeding the former as $S_\pi > S_O$. Of the rectangle OCDEB, the relevant area is OCDE.

For a point to the right of boundary BG, we find $\frac{P}{K} > \frac{\lambda}{S_\pi}$; this tells us that capitalists themselves are accumulating property (capital) at a rate exceeding that which is necessary to maintain the equilibrium path. Now, when this behavior is added to the rate of capital accumulation by workers, it means that the capital stock in total is growing excessively, and the equilibrium state breaks down. Insufficiency of aggregate demand can stem from over-zealous capitalist behavior. Therefore, the equilibrium value of the rate of profit cannot lie to the right of BG, it must lie on the relevant section of the boundary which is DE.

Regarding the other outcome, a point above the CF boundary shows:

$$\frac{Y}{K} > \frac{\lambda}{S_O}$$
$$\text{or} \qquad\qquad 7.80$$
$$S_O(\frac{Y}{K}) > \lambda$$

and, once again, we find (now in our one class society) that capital is being accumulated excessively. An equilibrium output to capital ratio must lie on the CD relevant part of the CF boundary.

If we take a point on the segment between D and E, and extend a line from it to C), we would show the condition:

$$S_\pi(\frac{P}{K}) = \lambda > S_O(\frac{Y}{K}) \qquad\qquad 7.81$$

179

capitalists' capital comes to dominate, and the distribution
of capital between the classes adjusts to present the growth
path as given by:

$$\frac{P}{K} = \frac{\lambda}{S_\pi}$$

7.82

It is S_π that matters; and while workers share in the profits
in proportion to the capital they accumulate, they are not
presumed to be sufficiently thrifty so as to by themselves
account for full-employment investment.

On CD, we find:

$$S_O(\frac{Y}{K}) = \lambda > S_\pi(\frac{P}{K})$$

7.83

Workers end up with doing all the accumulation; the steady-state
condition is their domain, and we have th dual outcome.

For a point inside the area OCDE, we have both $S_\pi(\frac{P}{K})$ and
$S_O(\frac{Y}{K})$ less than λ. Since capitalists property will be growing
at lower than the equilibrium rate, their share of total wealth
will approach zero; so that the steady-state outcome would be
that of the dual. But we see that this is not possible either,
as we still get an insufficient rate of capital accumulation.
A steady-state outcome will not exist.

Now we bring in the production function.

Fig. 7.4

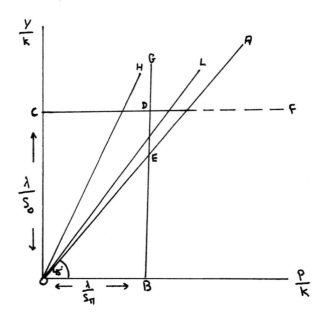

Fig. (7.4) shows the Cobb-Douglas function where we have unitary
elasticity of substitution and hence no change in factor shares.
Let the ratio of profits to income given by the function by the
line OH. We see that the steady-state solution cannot be given
by the behavior of capitalists. Thus:

$$S_{\pi}(\frac{P}{K}) < \lambda, \; S_0(\frac{Y}{K}) = \lambda$$

then:

$$S_{\pi}(\frac{P}{K}) < S_0(\frac{Y}{K}) \qquad\qquad 7.84$$

and:

$$\frac{S_0}{S_{\pi}} > \frac{P}{Y}$$

181

The savings of capitalists out of profits is insufficient, while savings of workers out of income is sufficient to yield the proper rate of capital accumulation.

Another way to reckon this is to write:

$$\frac{\frac{\lambda}{S_\pi}}{\frac{\lambda}{S_0}} = \frac{OB}{O_C} > OH \equiv \frac{P}{Y} \qquad 7.85$$

Should the ratio $\frac{OB}{OC}$ be equal to the profit share line, then the line OH would be drawn through the point D ($\frac{P}{Y}$ = OD) and the steady state solution could be given either way. But once off point D, the solution must be given in terms of $\frac{Y}{K}$ or $\frac{P}{K}$. And, the ratio of profits to income is insufficient to give the solution in terms of the rate of profit (the OH line is less than the required $\frac{P}{Y}$, since it has a greater slope than OD).

Howeverm should the income distribution be reflected in the line OL, we find:

$$S_\pi(\frac{P}{K}) = \lambda, \ S_0(\frac{Y}{K}) < \lambda$$

$$\text{and}$$

$$\frac{\frac{\lambda}{S_\pi}}{\frac{\lambda}{S_0}} < \frac{P}{Y} \qquad 7.86$$

with the ultimate solution $\frac{\lambda}{S_\pi} = \frac{P}{K}$.

What matters for the equilibrium outcome is the particular distribution of income in relation to the given savings propensities, and not any particular capital to output ratio.

Next we consider that the coefficients of production are fixed; the system exists with zero elasticity of substitution between capital and labor.

Fig. 7.5

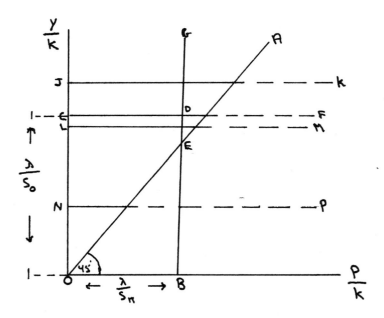

Fig. (7.5) shows three possible output to capital ratios (each given by a different production function), and we want to see which is compatible with what outcome. If $\frac{Y}{K} = OL$, then:

$$S_\pi(\tfrac{P}{K}) = \lambda \text{ (as LM cuts DE)}$$

or

$$\frac{\lambda}{S_\pi} < \frac{Y}{K}$$

and

$$\frac{\lambda}{S_O} > \frac{Y}{K}$$ 7.87

or

$$S_O(\tfrac{Y}{K}) < \lambda$$

183

An equilibrium solution exists with $\frac{\lambda}{S_\pi} = \frac{P}{K}$. The savings propensity of workers will not provide the full employment ratio of investment to output. As we can write from (7.8?):

$$S_O < \frac{\lambda K}{Y} = S_\pi(\frac{P}{Y})$$

and   7.88

$$S_O < S_\pi(\frac{P}{Y})$$

which is the Pasinetti condition.

Should $\frac{Y}{K} = OJ$, no steady-state solution is possible. From the view of the workers' society we find $S_O(Y) < \lambda K$, there is insufficient accumulation. And from the view that it is the capitalists' savings propensity that matters only, we see that JK relates to a rate of profit that is to the right of BG (it does not cut DE), with the result that capital will be accumulating at a rate in excess if the steady-state rate.

In the event $\frac{Y}{K} = ON$, again, no equilibrium solution is possible. Here the capitalists outcome provides insufficient accumulation, while the workers outcome provides too much.

It is interesting to note that if we presume fixed production coefficients, then for this to "permit" a steady-state solution, the output to capital ratio has got to fall within certain constraints given the savings propensities. The dual outcome is possible only if the output to capital ratio is equal to a particular value. For the Pasinetti outcome the requirement is less rigid. From (7.87) we have:

$$\frac{\lambda}{S_O} > \frac{Y}{K} > \frac{\lambda}{S_\pi}$$

and   7.89

$$S_O < \frac{\lambda Y}{K} < S_\pi$$

The output to capital ratio must be less than S_π but greater than S_0; and on the presumption of a large difference between these propensities, then the neo-Keynesian outcome will hold for wide flexibility in the capital to labor ratio. We now have a better appreciation of Pasinetti's point that his outcome is independent of the production function, though, it is not accurate to suppose that it is completely so.

Another possibility is where we suppose infinite substitutability between factors and no diminishing returns to earnings. For example, it is the rate of profit that is constant as the ratio of profits to output rises in proportion to the ratio of capital to output.

Fig. 7.6

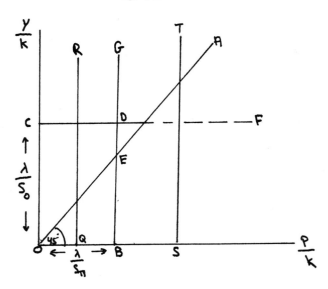

If the rate of profit is OQ, then the savings propensity of

capitalists matter too much, as we find $\frac{P}{K} < \frac{\lambda}{S_\pi}$; the steady-state
solution will then exist with $\frac{Y}{K} = \frac{\lambda}{S_0}$. A rate of profit given by
OS means no steady-state outcome at all. The TS line does not
cut CD, hence $\frac{\lambda}{S_\pi} < \frac{Y}{-}$; and it lies to the right of DE so that

$$\frac{\lambda}{S_\pi} < \frac{P}{K} \ .$$

At a prevailing rate of profit OQ, the system would have to
lower the ratio of capital to labor (raise $\frac{Y}{K}$) and thereby the
ratio of profits to income, if it is to bring about a condition
that can support the steady-state. This occurs, as we can see from
the diagram, when the property owned by capitalists tend to zero.
The dual solution is possible on the assumption that, for the
given S_0, the substitution of labor for capital, i.e. the change
in technique, can always accomodate the savings of workers. We
can suppose the savings propensity of workers to be at some reasonable
low level, and they would still be able to provide sufficient
to maintain full-employment. With this infinite substitutability
and no diminishing returns, the steady-state can be handled.

Yet equilibrium in this workers' society may founder on
this very assumption. While there may be some substitutability
of labor for capital, it is doubtful if it can be of sufficient
magnitude. At some point, the productivity of labor may be zero
or negative unless accompanied by additional (outside) investment.
One must not confuse hidden unemployment with productive full-
employment.

VI

Looking back over the neo-Keynesian road travelled in this
chapter, we have come to view the rate of profit and the distribution
of income as being determined by the basic forces of economic
growth; and have gotten away from the neo-classocal framework of the

186

technical nature of the production process and factor inputs.
A general comparison between these viewpoints regarding an
explanation of how income is distributed can be made as follows.[14]

Neo-Keynesian Theory:

Institutional factors determine a
historical division of income between
residual (capitalists) and non-residual
(workers) shareholders, with changes
in that distribution depending on
changes in the growth rate.

Neo-Classical Theory:

The distribution of income explained
solely by variable factor inputs and
the marginal productivity of those
variable inputs.

If we go with the Cobb-Douglas, we find the equilibrium outcome
independent of the production process. It is income distribution
that is integral to the explanation of growth. But if zero
substitution holds, then it is the production process that is
essential; what matters for the long-run outcome is the
particular output to capital ratio. Another way to approach
this is to say that neo-Keynesians assumed that savings behavior
was a long-run constant and explained growth via the particular
distribution of income; while the "neo-classical" view
assumed that the technical framework was constant, and then
explained growth via the existing savings behavior.

But it was really not the purpose of neo-classical theory
to explain growth; their effort was to explain income distribution
as such, and not as part of a wider growth context. So that if
we indeed find a low elasticity of substitution, then we ought
to put the neo-classical approach aside and concentrate on an
explanation of growth that will at the same time provide an

understanding of income shares. Now it is in this framework
that one can make reference to a neo-classical world in which
a production function plays a role, and a neo-Keynesian world
in which it does not. From the latter view, to reiterate, the
distribution of income and the rate of profit are not determined
as a function of any productivity of capital.

Perhaps a further clarifying point ought to be made here
concerning our distribution equation, which we repeat:

$$\frac{P}{Y} = \frac{1}{S_\pi} \cdot \frac{I}{Y} \qquad\qquad 7.90$$

If S_π < 1, the rate of profit comes to $\frac{\lambda}{S_\pi}$, and it is greater than
the rate of growth (as distinct from S_π = 1 and $\frac{S}{Y} = \frac{P}{Y} = \frac{I}{Y}$
with $\frac{P}{K} = \lambda$). The lower (S_π) the greater the amount of comsumption
out of profits which translates into lower consumption of
workers. Given the required growth of capital, then, as we can
see from (7.90), the lower S_π the greater would capitalists'
share have to be in order to maintain equilibrium. "There are,
then, two basic factors determining relative share of national
income: (a) the ratio of investment to total output and (b)
the propensity to consume out of profits."[15] We do recall
that our distribution equation is not upset when workers become
entitled to a share of the profits.

Note that in the condition S_π = 1, the maximum growth rate is
set by the minimum level of real wages (maximum rate of profit);
but when S_π < 1 (still S_0 = 0) the highest possible growth rate
will be set lower. The share of profits will not exceed that
set by the lowest acceptable real wage. And when S_0 > 0, S_π < 1
equilibrium is maintained when the growth rate is such as to
require that $(\frac{I}{Y})$ be greater than S_0 but less than S_π.

188

VII

It seems that control over investment suggests control over the distribution of income; the larger the rate of investment by the capitalist class the larger its share of the national output. Policy designs to achieve a more favorable distribution may be inconsistent with investment policies to maintain an equilibrium growth pattern. What neo-Keynesianism has done, by forcing distribution theory out of the static equilibrium mold, is to open the way for a study of these conflicting pressures. Let us say between a lower growth rate and a greater proportion of income going to workers, and a higher growth rate that, while it means an increasing level of income going to workers, results in their having a lower share of the national income.

We want to enlargen our hold on this relatively new neo-Keynesian paradigm by seeing what happens when the approach is updated, and the savings propensity of the capitalist class becomes that of the corporate sector of the economy.

1. N. Kaldor, "A Model of Economic Growth," *Economic Journal*, Dec. 1957.

   N. Kaldor and J. A. Mirrless, "A New Model of Economic Growth," *Review of Economic Studies*, June, 1962.

2. $$\frac{\frac{(Y_t - Y_{t-1}) \cdot K_t}{Y_{t-1}}}{Y_t} = \frac{Y_t - Y_{t-1}}{Y_{t-1}} \cdot \frac{K_t}{Y_t}$$

3. N. Kaldor, "A Model of Economic Growth," *Economic Journal*, Dec. 1957. Reprinted in Kaldor's *Essays on Economic Stability and Growth*, p. 266.

4. The stability of the equilibrium condition rests on the slope of the $\frac{S}{Y}$ curve exceeding the slope of the $\frac{I}{\Phi}$ curve. That is:

$$\frac{d(\frac{I}{Y})}{d(\frac{P}{Y})} < \frac{d(\frac{S}{Y})}{d(\frac{P}{Y})}$$

relating that $S_p > S_W$. The higher S_p, the smaller the fraction $\frac{1}{S_p - S_W}$, and the smaller the change in prices and the profit share stemming from a change in the investment ratio. This leads to smaller induced changes in the share of investment; we do not get cumulative increases in the profit share. On the other hand, the smaller S_p, the less the degree of stability following upon a change in the investment share. The smaller the difference between S_p and S_W, the larger $\frac{1}{S_p - S_W}$; and an increase in $\frac{I}{Y}$ will cause relatively large increase in the profit share that stimulates still larger changes in $\frac{I}{Y}$. Should $S_p < S_W$, there is then no chance at stability. Professor Kaldor refers to the term $\frac{1}{S_p - S_W}$ as the coefficient of sensitivity of income distribution. See his distribution in "Alternative Theories of Distribution," *Review* of Economic Studies, XXIX, 1962, pp. 267-79.

6. Ibid.,p. 276 (note 1)

7. Paul A. Samuelson, Franco Modigliani,"The Pasinetti Paradox in Neo-Classical and More General Models," Review of Economic Studies, XXXIII, 1966, pp. 269-301.

8. Ibid.,p. 274.

9. See N. Kaldor, "Marginal Productivity and the Macro-Economic Theorie of Distribution," Review of Economic Studies, XXIII, for an appraisal of these numbers,

10. Luigi L. Pasinetti, "New Results in an Old Framework," Review of Economic Studies, XXXIII, 1966, pp. 303-6.

11. Ibid., p. 304.

12. E. Helmstader, "The Long-Run Movement of the Capital-Output Ratio and of Labour's Share," Models of Economic Growth, Edited by Mirrlees and Stern, Halsted Press, 1973, pp. 1-17.

13. Based on J. E. Meade's work in his "The Outcome of the Pasinetti Process: A Note," Economic Journal, LXXVI, pp. 161-5.

14. This is one of several points of comparison between these two schools put together in a summary table by A. S. Eichner and J. A. Kregel, in their informative essay on post-Keynesian theory. The essay appears in the Journal of Economic Literature, XIII, Dec. 1975, pp. 1293-1314.

15. Ibid., p. 1298.

8. A FURTHER UNDERSTANDING[1]

We recall that the fact of $S_0 > 0$ makes no difference insofar as the aggregate ratio of savings to output. Though workers do save a smaller proportion out of profits than do capitalists, when the savings of workers out of their wages is added to their savings out of profits, it results in their total savings being equal to what capitalists would have saved out of profits they distributed to workers. The added consumption by workers out of their profit income is exactly offset by savings out of their wage income; workers save the same fraction of their income regardless of whethere it comes to them in the form of profits or wages.

I

Since enterprise is organized as corporations, the capitalist is now the corporation. Now this entity earns profits part of which is "consumed" in the form of dividends and non-investment spending (e.g. advertising), and part of which is retained, i.e. saved. The receipients of these dividends may also receive wages, or they may be a class of people whose income consists solely of dividends and other asset yielding income such as rent and interest; let us refer to this latter group as rentiers to distinguish them from capitalists in the sense of an entrepreneural class.

As distinct from the previous discussion, workers and rentiers do not necessarily receive profits in proportion to the savings each contributes (i.e. proportion to the amount of capital owned). Corporations have a savings propensity (S_C) as reflected in the proportion of profits they retain. Consider the following illustration.

Assume that workers (and also rentiers - so let us link them ogether, giving a personal non-instutional class) should receive $100 in profits, but the corporation retains 20% of these profits; and that the (S_O) is 10%. Should workers have received the $100, they would have consumed an amount equal to $100 (1 - .10) = $90. As is, they receive $100 (1 - .20) = $80, but it can be supposed that they will spend an amount equal to what would have been their consumption had they gotten their due. They spend in excess of dividend income, perhaps in the confidence the income is there, being held on their behalf by the corporation. They do not have possession of this income but they behave as if they do. We have:

$$90 = x(80)$$

8.1

$$x = 1.125$$

workers are overspending their dividend income by 12.5%. This can be put as:[2]

$$(1 - S_O)100 = x(1 - S_C)100$$

and

$$x = \frac{1 - S_O}{1 - S_C} > 1$$

8.2

so that

$$S_C > S_O$$

It makes no difference as to the proportion of profits that the corporation wishes to retain, workers will overspend their dividend income by the exact fraction required to make their consumption equal to $(1 - S_O)P_O$.

Morevover, as Kaldor points out, "Once we allow spending in excess of dividend income there is no reason to confine such spending to workers. "Capitalists" also spend some part of their capital gains (or even their capital in the absence of such gains)."[3]

193

There are, then, shareholders who overspend their current
dividend income, retired people who overspend their retirement
income - consuming their accumulated savings - and there are
active workers who save a fraction of their salary and wage
income for retirement (via purchase of securities).

When we take the total "quasi-contractual" portion of income,
i.e. wage and salary income, fixed interest and rent, there will
be a net saving out of this income that provides a demand for
financial assets. And on the other hand, the amount of net
dissaving out of income (the consumption of capital gains to
overspend dividend income) sets up a supply of these assets. But there
is also an addition to the supply of securities resulting from
new securities issued by the corporate sector. Since in the
securities market prices will tend to the level at which the
market is cleared; there must be some mechanism to ensure
that the spending out of capital (or capital gains) just
balances the savings out of income less any new securities issued
by corporations. We have the following considerations.

Corporations, in addition to retaining a fraction (S_c) of
their profits, also issue new securities equal to a fraction (i)
of current investment spending; (i) reveals the fraction of current
investment which corporations decide to finance externally. Changes
in the quantity of securities supplied by the corporate sector is
then functionally related to the demand for investment goods, which
is gK (g = growth rate, K = capital), and the demand for external
finance to underwite the investment. Also, that active workers
will save a fraction (S_0) of their income for retirement, and so
long as the population is rising and income per capita is rising,
then total savings from this group will exceed the dissaving of
the retire population. Furthermore we have that shareholders
liquidate a fraction (X) of their securities in order to finance

194

consumption from capital gains (G).

Equilibrium in the securities market means that the demand
for securities must equal the quantity of new issues supplied
by corporations plus the sale of existing issues (securities).
Thus:

$$S_0 W = XG + igK \qquad 8.3$$

Since it is the market price of securities which equilibrates
supply and demand, we need to see the variable in the equation
which is responsive to the change in price.

Before looking into equation (8.3) let us be certain about
what constitutes net income and total savings by households
and firms. Income can be written:

$$Y + W + (1 - S_C)P + S_C P \qquad 8.4$$

(S_C is the proportion of profits retained by firms)

Total savings is:

$$S = S_0[W + (1 - S_C)P] + S_C P \qquad 8.5$$

But in keeping with the basic Kaldor presentation, the assumption
is that there is no savings out of profit distribution; all
savings done by "capitalists" is savings done by firms. The
important marginal propensity to save on the part of the capitalist
in formulating the growth path, is really a measure of corporate
investment policy and the availability of funds. Equation (8.5) is:

$$S = S_0 W + S_C P \qquad 8.6$$

Getting back to the market equilibrium condition, we find
that the new securities issued by the firms when added to the
dissaving on the part of the retired workers plus spending out of
capital gains, make up the available supply of securities that
is demanded by the investment of active wage-earners. The
supposition is that all savings out of wages will be used to

increase the demand for securities. Restating equation (8.3) as:

$$XG = S_OW = igK \qquad 8.7$$

tells us that spending from capital gains (or capital) balances savings out of income (total security demand) minus new issues of securities. In other words, given (X), there is capital gains which prompts the sale of securities at a volume which balances the market. But what influences a change in the market value of securities, (i.e. rate of interest)?

These gains vary not only with variations in dividends and earnings per share but also with the "valuation ratio" (v). This ratio is a relation of the market value of shares to the capital employed by the corporations. It is the book value or share value per asset.

Suppose we have 25 shares at a price per share of $2,00, and the employment of 100 machines. Then:

$$v = \frac{25 \cdot 2.00}{100} = \frac{\$50}{100} = .50 \qquad 8.8$$

each asset is, so to speak, worth 50¢ in shares. Now let the corporation increase its capital stock by 10%, and finance this solely from retained profits. The number of machines goes to 110, and the market value of shares rises by the same percent to reflect this increase in assets. We find:

$$V = \frac{\$55}{110} = .50 \qquad 8.9$$

The market value of shares has gone up by the increase in the corporation's assets multiplied by the valuation ratio; that is:

$$.50(10) = 5.00 \qquad 8.10$$

As the number of shares remains unchanged, the increase in market value is entirely due to the change in price. Thus:

$$G \equiv \Delta p = v\Delta K = vgK \qquad 8.11$$

For the market value of shares to have gone up by 10% from

$50 to $55, the price per share must then have risen by 10% from $2.00 to $2.20. In this case we find the increase in the value per share (the capital gains per share) is equal to the increase in the total market valuation.

But now let us go back to the beginning and suppose that the 10% increase in capital is one quarter financed by the issuing of new securities. If we have the price per unit of new machines equal to 1.00, the corporation would have to raise $2.50 in the market place. That is:

$$p\Delta N = (gK \cdot 1.00) \cdot (.25) = \$2.50 \qquad 8.12$$
$$p\Delta N = \text{value of additional shares (N)}$$

Given the price of $2.00 per share, the corporation has to market 1.25 shares. The value of new securities, to state this again, is:

$$p\Delta N = igK = \$2.50 \qquad 8.13$$

In this case we find a gain in total market valuation of $2.50 which is greater than the gain per share. There is a total valuation of $52.50, but an increase in numbers to 26.25 which gives a gain per share of $2.00. The increase in total valuation is spread over existing shareholders (which shows the capital gains of $5.00) and the purchasers of new issues (which reduces the gains by the value of these new securities). Overall, the change in the market value of securities is:

$$G = vgk - igk \qquad 8.14$$

From equation (8.3) we can write:

$$S_O W = X(vgK - igK) + igk \qquad 8.15$$

or

$$S_O W = X(vgK - igK) = igk \qquad 8.16$$

Furthermore, the savings equal investment equation is:

$$S_O W - XG + S_C P = gK$$

$$\qquad 8.17$$

$$S_O W - X(vgK - igK) + S_C P = gK$$

197

Net savings from the "household" (non-corporate sector)
plus retaind earnings from corporations provide the funds to
carry on investment. And that portion of investment expenditures
financed by retentions is:

$$S_C P = gK - igK$$

8.17

$$= gK(1 - i)$$

Restating equation (8.17) we have:

$$S_O(Y-P) - X(vgK-igK) + gK - igK = gK \qquad 8.19$$

and

$$S_O(Y-P) - X(vgK-igK) = igK \qquad 8.20$$

also:

$$S_O(Y-P) - X(vgK -igK) + S_C P = gK \qquad 8.21$$

and

$$S_O Y + (S_C - S_O)P - X(vgK-igK) = gK \qquad 8.22$$

As $P = rk$, we substitute into (8.20) and (8.22):

$$S_O Y - S_O rk - XvgK + XigK = igK \qquad 8.23$$

and

$$S_O Y + (S_C - S_O)rk - XvgK + XigK = gK \qquad 8.24$$

Dividing (8.23) and (8.24) by gK, gives respectively:

$$\frac{S_O}{g} \cdot \frac{Y}{K} - \frac{S_O r}{g} - Xv + Xi = i \qquad 8.25$$

$$\frac{S_O}{g} \cdot \frac{Y}{K} + \frac{(S_C - S_O)r}{g} - Xv + Xi = 1 \qquad 8.26$$

Equations (8.25) and (8.26) yield solutions:[4]

$$v = \frac{1}{X}\left[\frac{S_O}{g} \cdot \frac{Y}{K} - \frac{S_O}{S_C}(1-i) - i(1-X)\right] \qquad 8.27$$

$$r = \frac{g(1-i)}{S_C} \qquad 8.28$$

Equation (8.27) tells us that there is a particular

valuation ratio and consumption out of capital gains such that, when taken with the given savings propensities, will result in the savings of the non-corporate sector being sufficient to absorb the new securities issued by corporations. Looking again at equation (8.20) we note that $igK = gK - S_CP$. Along the steady-state path, the required growth of capital is now the result of corporate investment policy; and the savings necessary to finance this investment flows from the personal and corporate sectors. But the savings propensity on the part of the corporation relative to the growth of capital will determine the extent of new securities issued which, via the valuation ratio, effects the capital gains and thereby the net savings to finance the investment. The policy of corporations towards new issues (the i) effects net savings in addition to the given value of (S_0), via its effect on net consumption from capital gains (i. e. dissaving). Along the equilibrium path, there is a particular (v) – given i – which assures that the sale of securities (old and new) equals net savings of households.

II

If all of the investment is internally financed, then $i = 0$ and $gK = S_CP$. Hence $G = vgK$, and $S_0W - XG$ will establish security prices such that the demand by savers will balance the sale of securities by dissavers, so that net savings of the non-corporate sector will be zero. The equilibrium price is determined by the parameters (S_0) and (X) given (G). And the capital gains will reflect the increase in the capital stock, given the constancy of the valuation ratio. In this circumstance, the maintenance of equilibrium growth from the point of view of the availability of savings to finance the proper rate of investment expenditures, is independent of the household sector, and

199

the rate of profit is then also independent, as given by the
Pasinetti outcome:

$$r = \frac{g}{s_C} \qquad\qquad 8.29$$

Yet "workers" do benefit from this increase in capital by
the increase in the market value of their securities, and by
receiving a share of the increase in profits which, they overspend from the realized capital gains. But this induces an
increase in aggregate demand that poses an inflationary threat
to the existence of the steady-state condition. Even with a
proper investment policy the growth path could be undermined
as the economy is propelled to what Mrs. Robinson refers to as
the inflationary barrier. At some point the lower real wage
(resulting from higher prices due to the higher consumption
expenditure out of profits) will set up pressure to raise money
wages that will reduce the ratio of profits to money wages, and
thereby the basis for the continued proper investment expenditures.
This rise in money wages increase expenditures and prices, and
the inflationary spiral takes hold. As Mrs. Robinson puts it,
"Thre is then a head-on conflict between the desire of intrepreneurs
to invest and the refusal of the system to accept the level of real
wages which the investment entails; something must give way.
Either the system explodes in a hyper-inflation or some check
operates to curtail investment."[5]

There could be an internal check to the onset of the barrier
if the forced savings on the part of fixed income groups (they
cut real demand as their real income declines) eleivates some of
the upward pressure on commodity prices. But one can expect such
action to be overwhelmed by the strong reaction on the part of
active wage-earners to close off any decline in their real wages.
If this check is not to be counted on, then the barrier will have
to be avoided by firms having to be more conservative in distributing

profits. The equilibrium growth path will be one of changed composition in that there is a higher proportion of investment to consumption goods. But we have a lot to learn with regard to our being able to avoid inflationary pressures during periods of high economic growth.

In the equilibrium condition the valuation ratio is given, thus enabling us to determine net savings in the household sector; with the value of the ratio dependent on the parameters S_O, S_C, X and i. Note from equation (8.28) that the rate of profit is independent of the parameters (S_O) and (X), but it does depend on aggregate household savings to supply adequate finance, through the influence of (i) on capital gains via the valuation ratio. Along the growth path, aggregate non-corporate savings will adjust to match the degree of external finance undertaken by corporations. The household sector's net saving depends not only on its own savings propensity, but also on corporate policy towards now issues.

Let us assume that the issue of new securities plus the sale of securities by retired households and others consuming capital gains, is greater than the demand for securities as given by $S_O W$. We have an excess supply of shares; the price of securities would be driven down and the valuation would be lower. With a given propensity to consume out of assets (X), the dissaving on the part of retired households would fall and thus allow the savings on the part of active households to accommodate the total supply of securities. In the steady-state condition the capital gains are such as to motivate a level of consumption of capital that when added to the new issues will equal the demand for shares. But this equality does depend on the particular corporate policy regarding the degree of external finance. Of course, what strikes one about this entire approach, is that the equilibrium path does not, as Kaldor puts is "Postulate a class of hereditary capitalists with a special high savings propensity."[6]

We are considering the savings behavior of a type of economic instution rather than a class of individuals; and what this implies for the distribution of profits between parts of the society. A growth accompanied by a higher dividend rate implies a lower (S_C) and a greater degree of external finance. Now market conditions will accommodate this circumstance to the given savings propensities, but the path may still be undermined by the inflationary impact of this lower corporate retention rate. The stability of the growth path has to be reckon not only with the proper level of investment, but with how it is financed.

III

Having gone through the fundamentals of this neo-Pasinetti theme, we will now retrace our steps somewhat in order to set matters out a little differently.[7]

Fig. 8.1

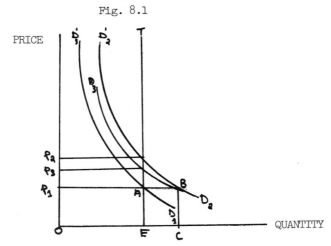

In fig. (8.1) we have TE stand for the supply of stock
of outstanding securities, and D_1D_1' for the demand curve
showing that people will want to replace money holdings with
securities as the price of securities fall. An equilibrium
price of P_1 will be established.

Let us have an increase in output from a level of investment that is financed totally from retentions. Given the
distribution of output between wages and profits, and the
savings propensity (S_0), then at p_1 there will be an increase
in the demand for securities as the demand curve shifts from
(A) to (B). This increase in demand is sufficient to absorb
additional securities at the p_1 price per unit, of an amount
equal to S_0W. If we also assume no consumption out of capital
gains, then this "bullishness" causes the price to rise to (p_2);
but it is a price that finds no actual change in the individual
portfolio holdings of the public. This is, what we can call,
an offer price only since no securities changes hands.

But realistically, there is some propensity to finance
consumption out of capital gains (XG). A value of $X > 0$ is
reflective of the shareholder realizing a "real-security balance
effect" when the market value of securities go up. Hence we can
propose a propensity to diminish holdings as their value increases.
On the one hand, a higher portfolio value reduces the demand
for securities which tends to dampen the higher value; while on
the other hand, the higher level of income stemming from the
investment which produced the higher portfolio value, increases
the demand for holdings with the resulting pressure for higher
prices. Of course, what we have is the market in operation, and
the price will settle below (p_2). Note in fig. (8.1) that the
release of securities dues to consumption out of capital gains
will cause the overall shift of the demand to be D_2BD_3. The

equilibrium price rises to (p_3); the result of what Professor Davidson refers to as the "net increase in bullishness of the public."[8] We make the point again, that at (p_3) though there is change in the portfolio balance of individuals, the public at large continues to hold the same quantities of securities.

In this world, the required investment to maintain equilibrium is equal to corporate savings, and that wage-earner household savings equates with household investment. One could assume away any inflationary pressures by postulating that household consumption expenditures is equal to the difference between full employment output and investment spending. But with a given distribution of income, consumption expenditures will be influenced by capital gains. A security market equilibrium price also becomes a mechanism for securing the necessary level of effective demand.

The issue of new securities by corporations can be shown with asupply flow curve that can be specified - with respect to the security price - by:

$$t = \frac{igK}{P} \qquad\qquad 8.30$$

$$t = \text{supply flow}$$

The total supply of securities consists of those in the portfolio of the public given as an inheritance from the past, plus new issues which is a function of the demand for external finance to underwrite investment. This total supply curve is seen in fig. (8.2).

Fig. 8.2

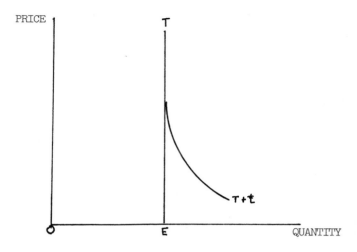

We combine this supply curve with the demand analysis of fig. (8.1)

Fig. 8.3

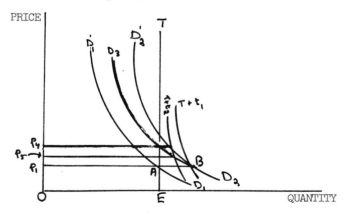

Should the amount of external finance required (at the p_1 price) equal savings (given S_0), then the increase in demand will be enough to absorb all the new issues. That is, the increase in the quantity of securities issued at the (p_1) price is equal to the increase in the demand for securities out of the given wage level at that price. The equilibrium price does not change, and the public in total simply adds to their possession of issues.

But should the desired external finance be less than savings $(S_0 W > igK)$, then the supply curve is $T + t_2$. The increase in the bullishness of households is not completely offset by new issues, so that the initial price (p_1) now rises to (p_4). What is happening is that the increase in demand is causing the price of securities to rise as they are being absorbed. Yet as prices rise, capital gains are realized, and shareholders then desire to liquidate some of their securities. This means, as we have shown previously, that the demand cuve slips over to $D_2 BD_3$ with the resulting equilibrium price rising only to (p_5).

The market price is the mechanism which causes the savings of households to be able to absorb all the securities offered. It is important to stress that the growth of the economy results from the decision on the part of the corporate sector to undertake a particular level of investment; while the flexibility of security prices assures that, given the distribution of income, the level of savings is available to finance it.

IV

We take another look at some of the relationships developed in this chapter.[9] Here we assume an economy in which all the inhabitants work and receive wages plus some income from profits (dividends $\equiv D$). Capital gains do not enter into this analysis, so that there is no consideration of it as part of income. Corporations decide whether net investment should be financed externally or by retained profits (thereby reducing the amount of profits paid out). We deal with a single household class (workers), with a propensity to save (S_O).

Household income (Y_O) consisting of wages plus dividends (D) is:

$$Y_O = wL + (1-S_C)P \qquad 8.31$$

But we can write $\beta = 1 - S_C = $ pay-out ratio by corporations; so $\beta = \frac{D}{P}$, and restate (8.31) as:

$$Y_O = wL + \beta P \qquad 8.32$$

Retained earnings (R) are:

$$R = S_C P = (1-\beta)P \qquad 8.33$$

with total income for the system being:

$$Y = Y_O + R = wL + \beta P + (1-\beta)P \qquad 8.34$$

If households do no saving (their average propensity to consume (b) equal unity) then all investment is financed from undistributed profits, i.e. corporate retentions. Aggregate savings is:

$$S = (1-\beta)P \qquad 8.35$$

Should b < 1, then total savings in the system comes to:

$$S = (1-b)Y_O + (1-\beta)P$$

$$8.36$$

$$1 - b = S_O$$

The disposal of income into consumption plus savings is written as:

$$Y = Y_O + R = b(wL+\beta P) + (1-b)(wL+\beta P) + (1-\beta)P \qquad 8.37$$

with the result:

$$Y_O + R = wL + P$$

$$\text{or} \qquad 8.38$$

$$Y_O = wL + P - R$$

We see that the pay-out ratio (β) affects the level of consumption (given b) and savings of households, and thereby the savings condition of the economy as a whole. Let us consider the one extreme of $\beta = 0$; then R + P and $Y_O = wL$. The consumption

level is at minimum because the level of income out of which
consumption flows is at minimum (corporations do not consume).
The consumption level as a proportion of household income is
higher than it is as a proportion of total income $(Y_0 + R)$.
And savings as a proportion of household income is lower
than out of total income.

As an illustration consider that (wL) and (P) are 150
and 50 respectively, and assume that $b = .80$. When $\beta = 0$,
wL · 150, and consumption spending is 120 which, as a proportion
of aggregate income of 200 gives a total propensity to
consume (b_T) of .60. Note that $b_T < b$. With $S_0 = .20$, household
saving come to 30 which, added to corporate savings (equal to P)
gives total savings equal to 80, and a total savings propensity
(S_T) of 140. Note that $_T > S_0$.

At the other extreme of $\beta = 1$, consumption is at a maximum
because household income is total income. We find $b_T = b = .80$
and consumption spending of 160. Also $S_T = S_0$ and savings
of 40.

Thus the lower the pay-out ratio, the lower b_T (which is
itself lower than b) and the higher the aggregate savings ratio
S_T (which is itself higher than S_0). For a given value of (b)
it is the level of (β) that, as we pointed out, determines the
thriftiness condition for the total system which will be of a
different value than for households (except in the case of
$\beta = 1$). A change in the value of (β) does not alter the level
of total income in the system, what it does is alter the household's
spendable income out of that total.

If $\beta = 1$ then, to repeat, $S_T = S_0$; and given the level
of investment chosen by corporations, it is the savings of the
household sector that must accommodate to maintain an equilibrium
conditon. The level of investment determines the level of income,

and hence the level of consumption expenditures given by
$(1-S_0)$ $(wL+P)$. Now should consumption be too high, i.e. the
capital sector is a higher proportion of total output than
savings is of household income; then for the given level of
money wages, prices and profit margins will rise. Since
$\beta = 1$, this effective demand is reinforced by dividends rising
by the same amount. "The effect of $\beta = 1$ is to recycle the
higher prices back in terms of higher dividends and it is
impossible to reduce the consumption value of income."[10]
With the given (S_0), changes in the level of profits will
have no effect on savings as a proportion of income, and the
economy exhibits explosive growth rates in output, if this
savings is less than investment. Thus the steady-state
path and the constancy of the rate of profit and income
distribution rests on the existence of a particular
household propensity to save.

When $\beta = 0$ there is maximum divergance between the household
and total savings propensities, as no part of household income
is attributable to profit distribution. Should desired investment
exceed savings now given by $S_0(wL) + R$ then, for the existing
money wage, profits will rise and with it the level of total savings.
We see a rise in output, prices and profits, but a fall in the
real value of money income. If money wages fail to keep pace with
inflation, we can expect that households will reduce their savings
propensity in an attempt to maintain real consumption levels. But
all this does is to accelerate the inflation, and the transfer of these
savings to the firm in the form of retained profits.

This inflation will lose its thrust when the level of savings
swells to equal the rate of investment; but here we are talking
about mainly an upper limit to retained profits. This can come
about due to the rise in the price level failing to keep pace with

the increased costs of doing business, and with the possibility
that households exhaust their capability to maintain real
consumption standards.

Our discussion recalls the role of the proper distribution
of income between household and firm in maintaining the
steady-state path. Given positive savings by households,
corporate retention must not be too low in relation to
planned investment. To put the matter another way: given
the level of investment necessary to maintain steady growth,
then for a value of (S_0), corporate profits must be a
particular portion of total income so as to result in an
aggregate value of savings equalling investment.

When $\beta = 1$, the equilibrium condition is given for a
particular savings propensity relative to the investment decision.
When $\beta = 0$, it is the proper distribution of income that matters
in order to extract the proper savings propensity relative to
the investment decision.

Should corporations distribute some of their profits in the
form of dividends, then the aggregate savings ratio is itself
determined by this very distribution. An increase in (β) increases
money income to households but less than in proportion; and the
value of (b) will determine the ensuing pressure on prices. Since
(β) does effect (S_T), then for the maintenance of the growth path
there has to be a rate of income growth such that given (β), there is
the equality of $S_T(Y) =$ Investment.

This pay-out ratio serves as a mechanism to maintain the proper
level of effective demand and profit margin. For a given rate of
investment, an increase in (β) will, depending on (b) and money wage
levels, bring about a higher rate of profit. And should investment
decisions be linked to the rate of profit, then, possibly, the
environment that would stimulate the proper investment could be had

if firms would distribute a greater share of their profits.
Let us make the point again, that in the equilibrium condition
the relationship of prices to costs are such as to yield a
level of profits that for the given (β), will result in the
savings – investment equality.

1. In this "Further Understanding" we look at, what Professor Kaldor refers to, as the Neo-Pasinetti Theorem. This is found in the appendix to Kaldor's article, "Marginal Productivity and the Macro-Economic Theories of Distribution," Review of Economic Studies, XXXIII, pp. 309-19.

2. See the illuminating discussion on this matter by G.C. Harcourt Some Cambridge Controversies in the Theory of Capital, Cambridge University Press, pp. 228-230.

3. Kaldor, op. cit.

4. Rearranging terms in (25) and (26) then subtracting gives:

$$-\frac{S_0 r}{g} - Xv = i - Xi - \frac{S_0}{g} \cdot \frac{Y}{K}$$

$$\frac{(S_C - S_0)r}{g} - Xv = 1 - Xi - \frac{S_0}{g} \cdot \frac{Y}{K}$$

then:
$$-\frac{S_0 r}{g} - \frac{(S_C - S_0)r}{g} = i - 1$$

and:
$$-\frac{S_C r}{g} = i - 1$$

$$r = \frac{g(1-i)}{S_C}$$

Sustituting the equation for (r) into (25) gives:

$$\frac{S_0}{g} \cdot \frac{Y}{K} - \frac{S_0 \frac{g(1-i)}{S_C}}{g} - Xv + Xi = i$$

then:
$$\frac{S_0}{g} \cdot \frac{Y}{K} - \frac{S_0}{S_C}(1-i) - Xv + Xi = i$$

and:
$$Xv = -i(1-X) + \frac{S_0}{g} \cdot \frac{Y}{K} - \frac{S_0}{S_C}(1-i)$$

so:
$$v = -[\frac{S_0}{g} \cdot \frac{Y}{K} - \frac{S_0}{S_C}(1-i) - i(1-X)]$$

5. Joan Robinson, <u>The Accumulation of Capital</u>, Irwin, 1956, p. 48.

6. Kaldor, op. cit.

7. Here we rely on part of Paul Davidson's analysis in his,
    "The Demand and Supply of Securities and Economic Growth
    and its Implications for the Kaldor-Pasinetti Versus
    Samuelson-Modigliani Controversy," <u>American Economic
    Review</u> (Papers and Proceedings) LVII, May, 1968, p. 252 -269.

8. Ibid., p. 260

9. Our analysis is based on Appendix D entitled "The Classless,
    Non-Income-Differentiated Model," in J. A. Kregel, <u>Rate of
    Profit, Distribution and Growth: Two Views</u>,Aldine, New York,
    1971.

10. Ibid., p. 217

9. A SUMMING-UP

In this chapter we want to return to the neo-classical model from which we set out, in order to catalogue its handling of matters in a comparison with the neo-Keynesian approach. There are certain aspects of neo-classicism that we found rather difficult to live with, and which prompted us to seek an alternative approach. Yet the model is consistent with those stylized facts relevant to industrialized countries over the last one hundred years or so.[1] The question, still open in the minds of some, is whether to consider the neo-classical or the neo-Keynesian paradigm as teh better (more realistic) simulation.[2]

Distributive Shares:

We begin with the neo-Classical approach. The economy applies the Cobb-Douglas function. Thus:

$$Q = Ae^{nt} K^{\alpha} L^{1-\alpha}$$

9.1

Q - physical output

A - multiplicative factor of production function

We find the marginal product statements.

$$\frac{dQ}{dK} = \alpha Ae^{nt} K^{\alpha-1} L^{1-\alpha} = \alpha \frac{Q}{K}$$

9.2

$$\frac{dQ}{dL} = (1-\alpha)Ae^{nt} K^{\alpha} L^{-\alpha} = (1-\alpha)\frac{Q}{L}$$

9.3

Profit maximazation equates the real wage with the physical marginal product of labor, hence:

$$\frac{w}{p} = (1-\alpha)\frac{Q}{L}$$

9.4

We have the marginal productivity of capital as:

$$\frac{dQ}{dK} = \alpha \frac{Q}{K}$$

9.5

Aggregate shares are:

$$L\frac{dQ}{dL} = (1-\alpha)Q \qquad\qquad 9.6$$

$$K\frac{dQ}{dK} = \alpha Q \qquad\qquad 9.7$$

We arrive at relative shares by dividing (9.6) and (9.7) by (Q):

$$\frac{L}{Q} \cdot \frac{dQ}{dL} = 1-\alpha \qquad\qquad 9.8$$

$$\frac{K}{Q} \cdot \frac{dQ}{dK} = \alpha \qquad\qquad 9.9$$

Now multiply (9.5) by the value of the capital stock (pK) and find:

$$\alpha\frac{Q}{K} \cdot pK = \alpha Qp \qquad\qquad 9.10$$

which defines profits (P). We know:

$$W = wL \qquad\qquad 9.11$$

W – wage bill

and

$$Y = W + P \qquad\qquad 9.12$$

Y – national money income

Arriving at the money wage rate from (9.4) and inserting into
(9.11) gives the wage bill as:

$$W = (1-\alpha)Qp \qquad\qquad 9.13$$

Inserting (9.13) and profits from (9.10) into (9.12) gives money
income as:

$$Y = \alpha Qp + (1-\alpha)Qp \qquad\qquad 9.14$$

We gave Y = Qp with distributive shares as:

$$\alpha = \frac{P}{Y} \qquad\qquad 9.15$$

$$(1-\alpha) = \frac{W}{Y} \qquad\qquad 9.16$$

Note that shares are derived without specifying anything about a
savings function; whether in terms of an overall propensity to

save out of aggregate national income, or in terms of different
propensities to save out of wages and profits, The neo-classical
view is to consider the aggregate propensity to save as a parameter
out of money income.

$$S = S(Y) \qquad\qquad 9.17$$

But if one considers the marginal productivity concept as
not a very meaningful explanatory device then one has to look
elsewhere to find distributive shares. The neo-Keynesian approach
does, as we know now, look elsewhere; it relies on a dis-aggregative
savings propensity with different ratios out of wages and profits
and a ratio of investment to output. Thus:

$$\frac{P}{Y} = \frac{1}{S_P - S_W} \cdot \frac{I}{Y} - \frac{S_W}{S_P - S_W} \qquad\qquad 9.18$$

If we hold the "classic" assumption $S_W = 0$, $S_P = 1$ then:

$$\frac{P}{Y} = \frac{I}{Y} \qquad\qquad 9.19$$

We can say that the higher the level of investment, or the
greater the rate of economic growth, the greater the share of
output going to the non-wage earner (assuming the simple notion
that the wage earner earns only wages). Yet on the realistic
assumption that some part of profits is spent on consumption
goods, we then have to write:

$$\frac{P}{Y} = \frac{1}{S_P} \cdot \frac{I}{Y}$$

$$\text{or} \qquad\qquad 9.20$$

$$P = \frac{I}{S_P}$$

reinforcing the notion that the more capitalists spend, the lower
S_P, the higher profits (capitalists get what they spend).

But we know that it is not the propensity to save out of a classification of income that matters, but the propensity to save by a classification of people (or by the corporation) that is central, so that we restate (9.20) as:

$$\frac{P}{Y} = \frac{1}{S_\pi} \cdot \frac{I}{Y}$$

Equality of Savings and Investment:
For a given propensity to save on the part of the capitalist, the overall propensity to save adjusts to support the full employment ratio of investment to output, based on the flexibility of distributive shares. From the neo-Keynesian viewpoint we have:

$$\frac{S}{Y} \equiv S_\pi \left(\frac{P}{Y}\right) = \frac{I}{Y} \qquad 9.22$$

As Professor Brems puts it, "In the Kaldor model the 'give' lies on the savings side. Here the overall propensity to save is a variable, hence capable of adjusting itself to any parametric propensity to save profits."[2] The distributive share is particular for the given steady-state outcome; a doubling of the savings propensity would be met with a halving of the ratio of profits to output. Thus in the neo-Keynesian world the adjustment is on the savings side; there is no change in the investment to output ratio which is, so to speak, determined from outside the system (perhaps by entrepreneurial expectations), given the rate of growth of the labor force.

Looking again at (9.21) we see one unknown $\left(\frac{P}{Y}\right)$ expressed in terms of growth of capital. We can view that equation as:

$$\frac{P}{Y} = \frac{\frac{K}{Y} \cdot \frac{\dot{K}}{K}}{S_\pi} = \frac{\frac{I}{Y}}{S_\pi} \qquad 9.23$$

In the simple steady-state outcome (no technological change) we have the equality of the growth rates for capital, output and that of the labor force. The solution for the profits share is given in terms of the rate of growth of capital which is not unknown in the context of the full-employment condition. Another view of the solution is:

$$S_\pi(P) = \lambda(\equiv\hat{K})K$$
$$\text{or} \qquad 9.24$$
$$r \equiv \frac{P}{K} = \frac{\lambda}{S_\pi}$$

In neoclassical analysis the overall propensity to save is not adjustable but is a given parameter; so that the give in the system has got to be the flexibility in the capital to output ratio. In a comparison of two economies exhibiting the same growth rate, but with one having twice as high a savings ratio than the othere, we will find that the higher ratio economy exhibits a twice as high degree of capital intensity and capital to output ratio. The higher savings ratio while not affecting the growth rate of the economy, does effect the level at which teh economy is proceeding steadily – the capital coefficient is now the variable. A higher savings ratio will transitionally cause capital and output to grow at a faster rate than the labor force; but when the full adjustment is made all variables are again growing at the same rate, but with a difference to reflect the changed savings rates (we have more capital employed and a lower ratio of output to capital). Also we will see a lower rate of profit and a higher wage rate.

We can write the matter as follows:

$$I = \hat{K}(K) \qquad 9.25$$
$$C = b(Y) \qquad 9.26$$
$$\begin{aligned} Y &= C + I \\ &= bY + \hat{K}(K) \end{aligned} \qquad 9.27$$
$$Y(1-b) = K(K) \qquad 9.28$$
$$\frac{K}{Y} = \frac{1-b}{K} \equiv \frac{S}{K} \qquad 9.29$$

A Neoclassical Investment Function:

What is happening is that in the higher savings rate system

we find a lower price of capital and a higher real wage rate.
The system will then respond to this change in factor prices
by altering factor proportions, i.e. the higher real wage will
induce a higher capital intensity. We can set out an investment
function analogous to the neo-Keynesian function of (9.22). Thus:

$$\frac{K}{L} = [(1-\alpha)A]^{-1/\alpha}(\frac{w}{p})^{1/\alpha} \qquad 9.30$$

The elasticity of capital intensity with respect to the real wage
is given by $(1/\alpha)$. It can also be shown that a higher propensity
to save results in a higher real wage by the expression:

$$\frac{w}{p} = [(1-\alpha)A]^{1/1-\alpha}[\frac{S}{K}]^{\alpha/1-\alpha} \qquad 9.31$$

which induces the greater investment ratio and capital intensity.

Is there sufficient factor proportion change in response to
relative price changes so that we lean towards the neoclassical view;
or are we dealing with fixed inputs along a growth path, and thereby
requiring that the system come up with that correct savings ratio
in support of it?

In chapters 7 and 8 we focused on the essential building blocks
of the new paradigm; we cam to this by way of our disenchantment
with certain neoclassical tools. Yet there is still controversy
as to whether neoclassicl theory can serve as a true desription of
real world events. Both camps construct aggregative models to come
to grips with the same complex reality (those Kaldorian stylized
facts). If this book has been helpful in clarifying these models
as a part of an ongoing understanding of the analysis of capital
accumulation, rate of profit and distribution, it will have served
its purpose.[3]

On closing this book, **I** would say that in the main the intellectual
battle is over. The Neo-Keynesians were right in their attack on
the Neo-Classical model, and they have defeated it on its own ground.

What looms in the battle for the classroom; to bring about a
change from the teaching of the comfortable "orthodoxy"
towards a restructuring of macro and micro courses (this
pedogogic distinction now appears all the more silly) that
account for the Neo-Keynesian developments.

NOTES

1. See the work by Professor Brems to show that the neoclassical model does explain the real world "as observed empirically." H. Brems, "Reality and Neoclassical Theory," _Journal of Economic Literature_, XV, March 1977. The format for our comparison of the neo-Keynesian and neoclassical models which makes up this chapter is based on two pieces by Brems. One is "Alternative Theories of Pricing, Distribution, Saving and Investment," _American Economic Review_, March 1979; and the other is "The Capital Controversy: A Cambridge, Massachusetts View of Cambridge, England," _De Economist_, 1975, 123(3). pp. 369-84.

2. Brems, _De Economist_, p. 372.

3. A good summary laying out the differences between the Neo-Ricardian (Neo-Keynesian) and Neo-Classical systems is found in Bentil Naslund and Bo Sellstedt, _Neo-Ricardian Theory_ (Lecture Notes in Economics and Mathematical Systems), Springer-Verlag. New York, 1978.